ENGLISH ⌗ HERITAGE

Book of
Chester

Peter Carrington

B.T. Batsford Ltd/English Heritage
London

© Council of the City of Chester 1994

First published 1994

All rights reserved. No part of this publication
may be reproduced, in any form or by any means,
without permission from the Publisher

Typeset by Lasertext Ltd, Stretford, Manchester
and printed in Great Britain by
The Bath Press, Bath

Published by B T Batsford Ltd
4 Fitzhardinge Street, London W1H 0AH

A CIP catalogue record for this book is
available from the British Library

ISBN 0 7134 7247 2 (cased)
0 7134 7312 6 (limp)

ENGLISH ⊞ HERITAGE

Book of
Chester

Contents

Illustrations

Colour Plates

Acknowledgements

Our first thanks go to Mr Peter Kemmis Betty, President of Batsford, and Dr Stephen Johnson of English Heritage for the invitation to write this book. The research on which it is based has largely been funded by Chester City Council, with substantial grant-aid from English Heritage and its predecessors.

Responsibility for the individual sections is as follows:

Peter Carrington – Roman invasion, the Roman fortress and Roman lead mining.

Gillian Dunn – Roman pottery supply.

Julie Edwards – leather industry.

Lesley Harrison – landscape.

Alison Jones – Holt.

Keith Matthews – Prehistory, the Roman civil settlement, early Saxon Chester

Michael Morris – Preface.

Dan Robinson (Museums Service) – Roman inscribed stones, the Saxon mint.

Simon Ward – late Saxon, Medieval and Civil War Chester.

Eileen Willshaw (Conservation Section) – Restoration, Georgian and Regency, Victorian and twentieth-century Chester.

Drawings – Peter Alebon, Cheryl Quinn, Timothy Morgan (private illustrator).

Index – Previn Karian (freelance editor).

Photographs – Simon Warburton (Museums Service).

Unless otherwise stated, contributors are staff of the City Council's Archaeological Service.

Peter Boughton of the Museums Service and staff of the City Record Office helped with the supply of historical illustrations.

The texts benefited from many helpful comments by members of the Chester Excavations Advisory Committee: Dr Lawrence Butler, Dr Ian Longworth and Mr Rhys Williams.

For permission to reproduce photographs we are grateful to the following:

The Dean and Chapter of Chester Cathedral

The Rector and Churchwardens of St John's Church

David Park of the Courtauld Institute of Art and English Heritage (Castle wall-paintings)

Cheshire County Council and the illustrator, Graham Holme (reconstruction painting of Leche House)

Chester Archaeological Society.

Photograph by W. Halford of the bronze statue 'A Celebration of Chester' reproduced by kind permission of North-West Securities.

For photographs taken inside commercial premises we are grateful for the co-operation of present and former occupants.

The project was managed for the Archaeological Service by Peter Carrington with help from Simon Ward. We are also grateful to Cliodhna Mulhern, Assistant Director (Cultural Services), Chester City Council, for her co-operation and to Dr Sarah Vernon-Hunt of Batsford for copy-editing.

Preface

This is the first book to look at the whole of Chester's history from an archaeological and architectural viewpoint. The invitation to write it could not have come at a better time, and it has given us the opportunity to reflect on what is distinctive and important about our city.

Chester has always been aware of its past. The Chester and North Wales Archaeological Society was established as long ago as 1849 and, together with the Chester Society of Natural Science, Literature and Art, founded the Grosvenor Museum in 1885. The running of the Museum was eventually taken over by the City Council, and in 1947 it was the Council who appointed Graham Webster – later, of course, to become an expert of international repute on the Roman army – as its first professional curator.

By the end of the 1960s it was clear that the city faced two threats: the physical decay of its old buildings and the obliteration of its archaeology through redevelopment of its historic centre. The City Council responded by appointing a Conservation Officer and then creating a field archaeology unit – one of the first in the country. Now, in the 1990s, we find ourselves in difficult times, and no activity, no matter how worthy, can be assured of funding. It is, therefore, perhaps a good time to make everyone aware of what is special about Chester's past.

It is true that Chester cannot claim to have the most impressive individual monuments compared to other English historic cities. Rather, its unique character lies in the fact that it preserves numerous buildings and monuments of a variety of periods in their original settings, rather than as islands conserved in a sea of modernity. Chief among these, of course, is the unbroken circuit of the City Walls, which incorporate elements from the Roman period onwards. Chester therefore meets the essential criterion for a textbook example of the development of an English city: its remains can easily be understood.

This special quality is something we wanted to convey in this book. The diversity of the city's heritage made it impractical for it to be written by a single person. We have therefore drawn upon the expertise of all members of the City Council's Archaeological Service. Very substantial and important contributions have also been made by staff of the Museums Service and the Conservation Section. In this way we have tapped the considerable fund of local knowledge that has been built up over the years.

We hope that reading this book enables you to understand and enjoy the city, and persuades you to visit it if you have not done so already.

Introduction

There is little evidence that Chester was a significant place in prehistoric times. The city owes its origin to its choice by the Roman army as the site for one of their legionary fortresses. The Romans recognized its strategic position, between North Wales and north-western England, guarding the lowest crossing of the river Dee and blessed with a natural harbour. This choice was confirmed by later generations, and so the city has been occupied continuously from Roman times onwards.

The centuries after the end of Roman rule are still dark ones. However, there are intriguing hints from documentary sources that Chester remained a place of some political significance, even though it may not have had a large population. It re-emerged as a place of national importance at the beginning of the tenth century, when it was refounded as one of a network of fortified towns during the reconquest of much of England from the Danes. It was also the English kingdom's window on to the thriving trading area of the Irish Sea. In order to finance this trade it had for a while one of the most productive mints in the country.

After the Norman Conquest the city held a key position on the Welsh border. It was for this reason that it was the seat of an earldom and that the county of Chester had semi-independent, palatine status. The city became the base for Edward I's conquest of North Wales. This attention from central government, and the wealth it brought with it, left its mark in the Castle, Walls and Rows.

Late in the Middle Ages there are reports of the Dee silting up, with the result that quays for larger vessels had to be built further and further down the estuary. The port of Chester did not finally die until the present century; but significant maritime trade long ago left the Dee and went to Liverpool. Nevertheless, the city continued to prosper quietly as a county town. In the absence of any important natural resources no large-scale industries developed, and consequently Chester did not grow into one of the major cities of England.

This alternation of periods of prosperity and stagnation is responsible for the remarkably complete preservation of some features from the city's past. The Saxon revival was late and came at a time when there was a revival in town-planning. This meant that much of Chester's Roman defences and street-plan survived through the 'Dark Ages' to find a new use. Likewise the city's lack of substantial growth since the late Middle Ages led to the survival of much of its medieval fabric until the heightened historical awareness of the nineteenth century ensured its preservation.

Ironically, it was much more recently, in the 1960s, that some of the greatest losses occurred. The commercial pressure to rebuild much of the city centre, combined with the increased destructiveness of modern building techniques, led both to the revelation of how much more still survived beneath the soil than had been imagined, and to its rapid and total destruction. It also led to the loss of some fine and much loved standing buildings. Fortunately, since then the city's past has been seen as one of its greatest assets and has been treated accordingly.

An account such as this inevitably tends to give the impression that everything is known.

In fact, this is very far from the case: the port area, the Roman extramural settlement, 'Dark Age' and Saxon occupation, and settlement in the neighbouring rural areas, are all topics where archaeological knowledge is patchy at best, and major questions remain even about the Roman fortress, which has been investigated in some detail.

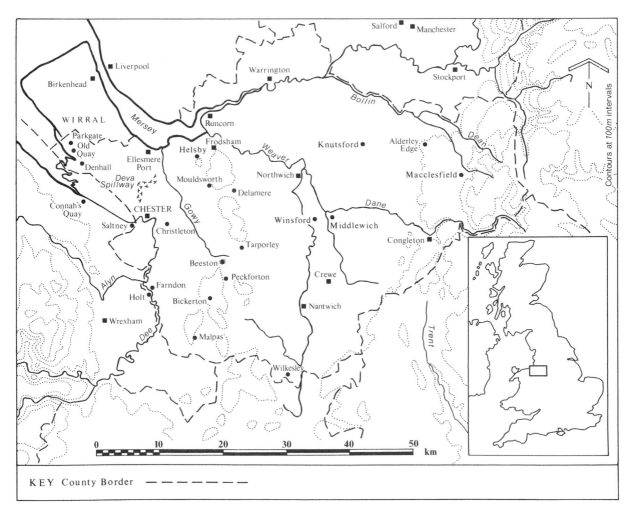

KEY County Border — — — — — —

1

The Cheshire Landscape

The county of Cheshire lies centrally in the western lowlands of England. Its traditional boundaries were defined by natural features. To the north lies the Mersey ('the frontier river' in Old English), which opens out abruptly from mosses – only crossed easily at Runcorn and Warrington – to a broad estuary. In the east the edges lie upon the foothills of the Pennines. The southern limit runs along the watershed of the Dee–Mersey and Severn–Trent river systems. In the west the boundary follows the course of the Dee, only crossing it to include a few parishes south and south-west of Chester; in the north-west it extends to the Wirral peninsula. The sandstone Mid-Cheshire Ridge, running from Helsby in the north, via Beeston and Peckforton, to east of Malpas in the south, divides the county into an eastern and western lowland. Apart from the Dee and the Mersey along its boundaries, the main river in the county is the Weaver, which rises west of Nantwich and flows north into the Mersey. The Gowy rises in a gap in the Mid-Cheshire Ridge and again flows north into the Mersey. Chester lies in the north-western corner of the west Cheshire plain, between 15m (50ft) and 61m (200ft) above sea level. In the local government reorganization of 1974 the county lost the 'panhandle' running into the Pennines east of Manchester and the northern half of the

1 *Map of present-day Cheshire, showing the main towns and post-1974 county boundary.*

Wirral, but gained Warrington and Widnes north of the Mersey.

Geology

The western Cheshire lowland is a faulted structural basin trending north-east to south-west. The solid rock outcrops as Bunter sandstones. Chester sits on a ridge of the harder Chester Pebble Bed Bunter sandstone. This ridge follows a north–south line through Chester and Farndon and rises to the north of Chester. Deposition of more clay-rich deposits formed the younger Keuper marls found in the eastern half of the county and the sandstone escarpments at Helsby and Bulkeley Hill. Salt beds formed near Northwich and Wilkesley.

The underlying parent rock is covered in many places by sands and gravels left by melting glaciers during the last two million years. During the last glaciation, ice advanced from across the Irish Sea up the Dee and Mersey estuaries. Local ice moved from the Pennines and Wales and pushed south towards the Midlands. When the ice finally melted, sands and gravels were liberated and the streams draining away the meltwaters cut new channels. The most impressive of these is the so-called 'Deva Spillway', just north-west of Chester, formed when the meltwaters from the eastern lowland of Cheshire flowed into the Mersey, but found its estuary still blocked by ice. They therefore cut a new channel to escape into the Irish Sea via the Dee. In so doing they

13

helped to give the Dee estuary the form it had until the river was eventually canalized in the eighteenth century.

Soils and agriculture

The parent rock affected the characteristics of the soil which formed above it. Sandy soils occur over the Mid-Cheshire Ridge, but elsewhere they are generally clayey. However, those overlying the Bunter sandstones of the western lowland are sandier, acidic and free-draining. They have good agricultural potential and provide almost year-round pasture. At present they support mixed open woodland dominated by ash and birch. Soils on the Keuper marls and sandstones are more stony and harder to work because they have a higher clay content which impedes drainage. Only areas of upland in the east of the county, where peats formed, have poor agricultural potential and are regarded as marginal.

Raw materials

Rock salt in the Northwich area was a commodity exploited at least from Roman times on a small scale. Salt was mined in the Norman period, but the industry only expanded in the eighteenth and nineteenth centuries with improved transport along the new canal network.

Metal ores such as copper, lead and cobalt in the Alderley Edge and Bickerton areas were exploited in pre-Roman times, although evidence of large-scale extraction is scanty until the later seventeenth century.

Lines of communication

Communication routes have been conditioned by geological features and river drainage patterns. Early man found it easier to move along sparsely wooded ridges and river valleys than through thick woods. Early lines of communication would have been from the north, across the Irish Sea up the Dee estuary, and south through the Midland Gap. Gaps in the Mid-Cheshire Ridge carved out by the glaciers allowed easy east–west movement. For example, the salt route from Nantwich to Wales made use of the gap in the Bickerton Hills. The path of the river Gowy at Beeston also follows an old glacial drainage channel; the same route is now used by the railway line from Chester to Crewe.

The river Dee

The course of the Dee around Chester has changed dramatically in historical times, as is visible in old maps, where the river can be seen flowing at the foot of the now-dry Water Tower. The early estuary would have been wide, sheltered and shallow. It lacked the tidal scouring and shifting shoals of the Mersey. Over the years natural erosion caused the accumulation of sand and silt. This silting was accelerated by the clearance of marginal uplands within the watershed, which increased soil erosion. Silting was recorded in the Middle Ages, but only became a serious problem in the seventeenth century. To cope with it, a series of small ports was established nearer to the estuary mouth, and eventually the river was dredged and recut to restore the deep-water channel. This diverted the channel to the Welsh side of the estuary. Silting continued and the tidal reaches on the Cheshire side receded, allowing land to be reclaimed at Saltney and Sealand.

The selection of settlement sites

When the last ice was retreating, the landscape was open, exposed tundra, with stunted trees such as dwarf birch. As the temperature rose, willow and juniper became established. Pine began to spread northward into Cheshire and with birch formed the pre-Boreal forests of the early post-glacial period. Climatic improvement in the Boreal period allowed hazel, elm, oak and lime to become established in a time of warm dry summers. Although still warm, the climate became wetter around 5000–4000 BC. Oak dominated the mixed woodlands on the clay soils, while on the drier sandstone soils sessile oak was more abundant. Ancient woodlands are rare, but Peckforton may have been wooded since the end of the last ice age. Man modified the environment and clearance increased peat formation in the uplands. Peat had already begun forming as a result of a wetter climate in glacial hollows and areas of impeded drainage such as valley bottoms.

Natural features such as relief, lines of communication, vegetation cover, water supply and raw materials particularly affected the choice of settlement sites before the Roman conquest. The general pattern seems to be that areas of sandstone escarpments and ridges were favoured because they were easier to clear than the densely-wooded valleys. The higher ground also provided lines of communication. With technological advances the lower-lying, wooded ridges of the Chester Pebble Beds and Kinnerton sandstones in the west could be cleared for settlements.

2

Cheshire in Prehistoric Times

It used to be a commonplace that Cheshire had virtually no prehistory as it had clay soils, unsuitable for early agriculture, with large areas of marsh and dense woodland, making only a sparse population possible. This picture is beginning to change, with a significant number of finds ranging in date from the Palaeolithic (the Old Stone Age, before about 11,000 BC) to the eve of the Roman conquest in the second half of the first century AD.

It has long been recognized that the 'Three Age System', which classified the prehistoric period according to technology (i.e. stone, bronze and iron), is not the best way to look at the period. This is particularly true in the north-west of England, where it is not possible to distinguish between the Late Bronze and Iron ages. In this chapter prehistory has been divided according to social complexity. The earliest societies were bands of hunter-gatherers, mobile communities whose members were probably all related. After the introduction of farming in the fifth millennium BC societies became more settled and tied to the land. They began to develop territorial identities and built complex monuments to express and reinforce those identities. Around 1250 BC a major change occurred, which led to the construction of massive hilltop enclosures (hillforts) and the abandonment of upland domestic sites. It is these three broad divisions which have been used here.

Hunters and gatherers (before c. 4500 BC) (2)

The Palaeolithic (Old Stone Age)

We do not know when human beings first arrived in the Chester area. For much of the period, in common with the rest of northern England and Wales, it was covered by ice which at its maximum was about 450m (1500ft) thick. Its retreat began in the south-east of the county about 18,000 years ago.

There are no securely dated early prehistoric sites in the area covered by this book. Some 50km (30 miles) to the west, at Cefn Cave in Clwyd, the remains of Neanderthal-type humans and their tools have been found in deposits dated to 225,000 years ago. To reach this spot the hunting group must have passed through Cheshire during the warm phase known as the Hoxnian Interglacial.

At Carden, 13km (8 miles) south of Chester, a few artefacts of chert and flint have been found (3). Some of them appear to date from the Upper (or Later) Palaeolithic (35,000 to 11,000 BC), but more unusual are the rock shelters in a cliff also at Carden. They overlook the Dee valley and lay on a migration route for herds of game animals moving from winter pasture in south-eastern England and northern France to summer pasture in the Welsh Marches. The shelters were perhaps used seasonally in early and late summer by small groups of hunter-gatherers.

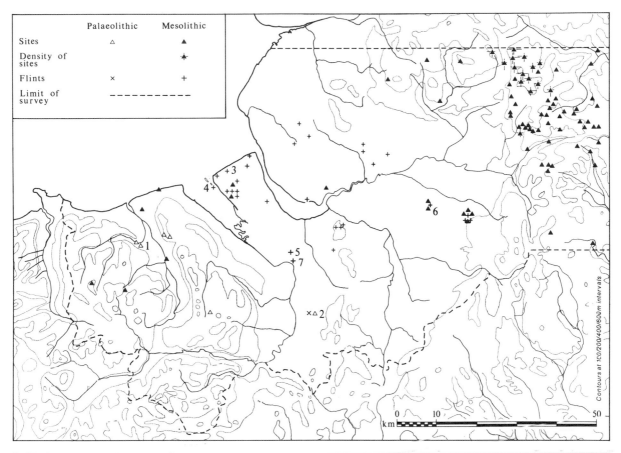

2 *Early prehistoric Cheshire. This map spans 200,000 years, from the first visits by hunter-gatherers in the Ice Age to the beginnings of permanent settlement by 4500 BC. The coastline is the modern one.*

Key
1 *Cefn Cave*
2 *Carden rock shelters*
3 *Meols*
4 *Hilbre Island*
5 *Bache Pool*
6 *Tatton Park*
7 *Chester, Lower Bridge Street*

3 *Chert tools from Carden. These crude Upper Palaeolithic tools show that visiting groups of hunter-gatherers camped here before the end of the Ice Age.*

The economy of hunter-gatherers was based largely on the collection of wild plants, including roots and berries. This was supplemented by hunting for fish, birds and small mammals. The hunting of big game animals was probably not important to the diet, although a single kill would obviously have provided a great deal of meat, bone for tools and hide for clothing, containers and so on.

17

The Mesolithic (Middle Stone Age)

It was in the Mesolithic period, from about 11,000 BC, that the first permanent settlers arrived in Britain. Flint scatters of this date have been found on the western slopes of the Mid-Cheshire Ridge. From settlements on its top or its slopes, the marshy river valleys of the Gowy and Dee to the west and the Cheshire Plain to the east were within easy reach. These locations offered the Mesolithic hunter-gatherers access to a great diversity of plants and animals.

There were at least three important sites on the Wirral peninsula during the Mesolithic. The enigmatic settlement at Meols, near Hoylake at the northern tip of the peninsula, was explored in the nineteenth century. Although the actual site has now been washed away by the sea, the antiquarian collections of material from it demonstrate occupation at all periods

from the Mesolithic through to the thirteenth century AD. Hilbre Island, off the north-western tip of Wirral, has also produced a good collection of Mesolithic material.

4 *The first farmers in Cheshire* (c. *4500–1250* BC). *These people colonized the low-lying, rich agricultural land during the Neolithic period and expanded on to the poorer uplands during the Bronze Age. The coastline is the modern one.*

1 *Congleton, The Bridestones*
2 *Somerford long barrow*
3 *Churton mortuary enclosure*
4 *Carden barrow cemetery*
5 *The Calderstones*
6 *Kelsall cremation*
7 *Jodrell Bank barrow cemetery*
8 *Seven Lows barrow cemetery*
9 *Bickerton copper source*
10 *Alderley Edge copper mines*
11 *Bridgemere hoard*
12 *Beeston*

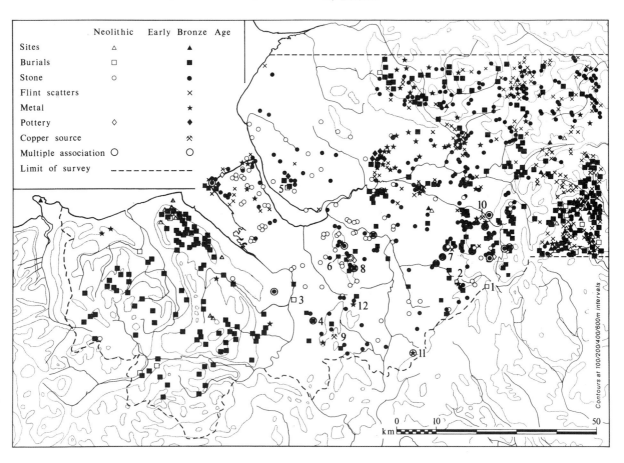

The third site, the Bache Pool, lies 1.5km (1 mile) north of Chester. When the pool was drained in the nineteenth century a collection of Mesolithic microliths was discovered. These are small geometric flints designed to be slotted into a wood or bone handle. The collection also includes at least one core from which blades to make the microliths had been struck.

The site, by the side of a small pool or 'mere', is very like one excavated at Tatton, in the east of the county. At both sites the mere had developed from a small stream in a marshy valley during the Mesolithic period; a hunter-gatherer group had camped beside it for the food it offered, including fish, water-fowl and aquatic mammals such as beavers.

5 *The Bridestones, Congleton. These are the remains of the stone walls of a Neolithic 'chambered tomb'; the mound which originally covered them has long since been destroyed.*

The first farmers (*c.* 4500–1250 BC) (4)

The Neolithic (New Stone Age)

In the middle of the fifth millennium BC, the first farmers arrived in Britain from the continent of Europe in search of new land to cultivate, bringing with them crops and animals. The changes they brought to the landscape and economy were so disruptive and indeed irreversible that the hunter-gatherer communities eventually had to adopt the new practices. The Neolithic of Cheshire has few impressive monuments to compare with the long barrows and causewayed enclosures of other parts of the country. The Bridestones near Congleton (5) are the denuded remains of the county's only chambered tomb, a typical Neolithic method of communal burial; there is also a possible earthen long barrow at Somerford. There are no other upstanding monuments of the period.

A third Neolithic site has been identified from aerial photographs at Churton, south of Chester. It consists of a roughly rectangular enclosure with an entrance to the south. This was probably a mortuary enclosure, a place where corpses were left to decay. It would have had an internal timber structure in which the burials were deposited. Some Native American peoples and South Sea Islanders practised similar methods for the disposal of their dead. Such burial practices are thought to show a society with few, if any, class distinctions.

Burial mounds and mortuary enclosures are believed to have formed the focal points of social territories. The Bridestones were perhaps the focus for a group living on the western flank of the Pennines, the Somerford long barrow for a group on the central Cheshire Plain and the Churton mortuary enclosure for a group living in the Dee valley. North of the Mersey the Calderstones were the remains of another chambered tomb, now destroyed. There are probably more burial sites awaiting discovery.

Neolithic flint scatters have been found all over Cheshire, with polished stone axes and pottery adding to the list of finds. The rock-shelters at Carden have produced a chert scraper of probable Neolithic type.

The Early Bronze Age

The transition from Neolithic to Bronze Age, around 2450 BC, was a gradual one. Bronze tools did not immediately replace flint or stone, and must have remained a costly luxury for many centuries. During the late Neolithic, society had become increasingly stratified, and this trend was reinforced by the arrival of bronze, the use and control of which must have fallen into the hands of a few wealthy people. This stratification is reflected in the change from communal burial in the Neolithic to the single burial of apparently privileged individuals in the Bronze Age.

The source of the copper needed to make bronze was probably the vein which runs along the eastern flank of the Mid-Cheshire Ridge. It was mined commercially at Bickerton during the nineteenth century, and it is quite probable that it was quarried in prehistoric times. There is also Bronze Age copper mining at Alderley Edge, in the east of the county.

Round burial mounds, or barrows, are the most common monument of the Early Bronze Age (c. 2450–1250 BC). Although Cheshire does not have a large number of surviving mounds by national standards, almost a hundred are known, mostly in the east of the county. In addition there are cremations without mounds, such as one found at Kelsall, 12km (7$^1/_2$ miles) east of Chester (**6**).

At Carden, close to the earlier rock shelters, five round barrows were levelled during the nineteenth century. Although not recorded in detail they appear to have formed a cemetery similar to ones at Jodrell Bank and Seven Lows. A sixth mound at Carden survives as an earthwork.

Many stray finds of objects dating from the earlier Bronze Age have been made throughout the region, particularly axes and palstaves, although none come from Chester itself. The best group comes from a hoard found at Bridgemere in the south of the county, but recent finds by metal-detectorists and walkers have a marked tendency to cluster around the Mid-Cheshire Ridge.

Three axe-hammers have been found at Beeston. They seem to have been status symbols rather than tools and may show the growth of a class of more 'wealthy' individuals. These axe-hammers are the first evidence of occupation at the important site at Beeston which continued in use throughout later prehistory and into the Middle Ages.

Late prehistory (c. 1250 BC–AD 60): social change and the growth of social complexity (7)

The Late Bronze Age and Iron Age

The later Bronze Age seems to have seen some sort of social upheaval. By about 1250 BC human remains were no longer being buried as a means of disposal, and many upland settlements were deserted. This desertion was due partly to a worsening climate, but also to over-intensive farming, which had exhausted the soil. Around the same time, or perhaps a little later, large hilltop enclosures or hillforts (to use their common, but inaccurate, description) were constructed.

A string of hilltop enclosures runs along the Mid-Cheshire Ridge, starting at Helsby Hill in the north, through Eddisbury and Kelsborrow Castle at Kelsall, to Maiden Castle at Bickerton. In addition there are several smaller promontory enclosures, including one at Burton Point, Wirral. Beeston was also occupied, with an enclosure where the castle's outer bailey ditch runs. Excavations there have located a bronze-working hearth together with fragments of crucibles and moulds. The metalwork associated with the hearth is of a Late Bronze Age type, dating from about 1000 BC, but metalworking perhaps began there much earlier.

None of the other enclosures has been subjected to modern scientific excavation, and little is known about their date and function. It is usually assumed that they were still occupied at the time of the Roman invasion, but there is no proof of this. They are thought to have been centres of power, the residences of individuals whom we could reasonably call chieftains. Their defensive nature points to unsettled conditions, perhaps because the desertion of marginal lands created a refugee problem or a crisis in land ownership.

The only finds in the region which can be dated to later prehistory are a few sherds of so-called 'Very Coarse Pottery' from some of these enclosures and from the rampart of the Roman

fortress at Chester, a few scraps of metalwork, a couple of Iron Age pins and some coins from Meols. No domestic pottery of this date has yet been identified, and this has been a major handicap in locating more occupation sites.

Very Coarse Pottery has been recognized as a specialized industrial type used in the

6 *Middle Bronze Age burial from Kelsall. The 'collared urn' is typical of cremation urns of this period (c. 1700–1250 BC), and was found in the centre of a ring of kerb stones.*

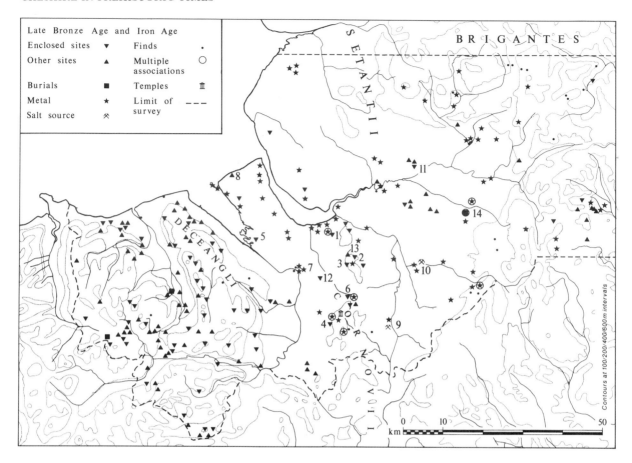

7 *Cheshire in later prehistory (c. 1250 BC–AD 60). This map shows the Late Bronze Age abandonment of the uplands and the beginnings of tribal organization. The coastline is the modern one.*

Key
1 *Helsby Hill*
2 *Eddisbury*
3 *Kelsborrow Castle*
4 *Bickerton, Maiden Castle*
5 *Burton Point*
6 *Beeston*
7 *Chester*
8 *Meols*
9 *Nantwich*
10 *Middlwich*
11 *Great Woolden Hall Farm*
12 *Waverton*
13 *Kelsall, Longley Farm*
14 *Lindow Moss*

production and distribution of salt. Its source is, predictably enough, the Nantwich–Middlewich salt-producing area. By the fifth century BC this type of pottery was being traded as far afield as the Wrekin in Shropshire and North Wales, although no direct evidence has yet been found for pre-Roman salt-production in Cheshire.

In other areas of Britain the Iron Age saw a continuous population growth, with the most rapid expansion during the first century AD, on the eve of the Roman invasion. More farmsteads were established and the landscape was opened up. This agricultural intensification has only recently been recognized in Cheshire, and there are hints of it in Merseyside and Clwyd. In Greater Manchester an enclosed settlement has been excavated at Great Woolden Hall farm; it was founded in the Late Iron Age and continued in use after the Roman Conquest. It is typical of sites known from aerial photographs throughout the region, and has a parallel at Waverton, 5km (3 miles) south-east of Chester.

Excavations in Chester have produced little evidence for pre-Roman activity. Plough marks have been preserved beneath the parade ground at Frodsham Street, outside the legionary fortress; their dating is not certain but is usually assumed to be late Iron Age. Another site, at Eastgate Row in the city centre, has slight traces of domestic rubbish in a deposit earlier than the establishment of the Roman fortress. We can be certain that someone was living and farming here in the middle of the first century AD, but we do not know who they were or what sort of settlement they inhabited.

Although only a few Iron Age objects have been found at Meols, they are extremely interesting. Three silver Carthaginian coins, two silver coins from Brittany and one gold British coin hint at wide-ranging trading contacts. They bring to mind the important trading settlement at Hengistbury Head, on the south coast east of Bournemouth, which was a major port and centre for redistribution. It may be suggested that minerals – lead and silver – from North Wales were the principal objects of trade, but furs, wool and slaves are also possibilities. The quality of the material found at Meols suggests some form of economic and, by implication, political control, because long-distance trade, however sporadic, needs to be managed. This is unlikely to have been as complex as in the emergent states of south-eastern Britain; Cheshire was a peripheral zone and did not yet, for example, have its own coinage. Nevertheless, the Late Iron Age was a period of rapid economic and political growth and profound social change in Britain generally and it is possible that the local elite was on a path of increasing complexity when the Romans arrived.

The best known Iron Age find from Cheshire is the bog body from Lindow Moss. Radiocarbon dating has produced a wide range of results and so we cannot be certain about the exact date of the body, but many archaeologists would prefer to assign it to the first century AD. The man had been killed by a blow to the back of the head and had been garotted and had his throat cut before being thrown into the bog. Parts of other human bodies have been found during peat-cutting at the Moss, as elsewhere in the British Isles and northern Europe. These bodies may be the victims of human sacrifice, and it appears that Lindow Moss was the focus of some fairly gruesome ritual activity in the centuries before the Roman invasion.

Cheshire on the eve of the Roman invasion

There are few indications of what was happening in the region at the time of the Roman invasion. There are no known settlement sites apart from Meols, and possibly Waverton, and the hilltop enclosures. There is a possible 'Celtic' field system at Longley, near Kelsall, but this may be later in date. A few stray finds such as brooches may also derive from Iron Age farmsteads, but until there are excavated sites and dated artefacts we cannot be certain about the economy or society of late Iron Age Cheshire.

Nor is it clear how the region was organized politically in the first century AD. In Roman times Chester lay within the territory of the tribe known as the Cornovii. However, the centre of their tribal power lay at the Wrekin in Shropshire, and it is possible that large parts of Cheshire were controlled either by a separate tribe or by a sub-group of the Cornovii. We know that the west bank of the Dee estuary lay in the hands of a tribe called the Deceangli, and it is possible that they controlled the entire estuary, including Wirral, and perhaps large parts of the Dee flood plain. It is also possible that eastern parts of the county were controlled by a sub-group of the Pennine tribe of the Brigantes. Archaeology, unfortunately, has not yet shed any light on these problems.

3

Roman Chester

The Roman invasion of Britain

The Roman conquest of Britain was begun by the emperor Claudius in AD 43. The invasion force consisted of four legions: II *Augusta*, IX *Hispana*, XIV *Gemina*, and XX (later to carry the titles *Valeria Victrix*) – about 20,000 men – and an equal number of auxiliaries. Each legion consisted of 5000–6000 men, almost entirely infantry. Recruits had to be Roman citizens and so tended to come from the older and more civilized parts of the empire. The auxiliary units, on the other hand, were smaller, 500 or 1000 strong. They could be infantry or cavalry and were recruited from non-citizens in the less advanced or newly-conquered parts of the empire.

Much of the literary evidence for events in the years up to the foundation of Chester is provided by the Roman historian Tacitus in three works, the *Annals*, the *Histories* and the *Agricola*. The last is a biography of his father-in-law, Gnaeus Julius Agricola, who was governor of Britain in the years 77–84 and is mentioned on inscriptions from Chester. Unfortunately what Tacitus reported were merely isolated highlights. The archaeological evidence for the Roman campaigns comes from numerous military sites, some partly excavated, many only recorded by aerial photography, and matching this with the literary evidence can sometimes be difficult.

There is most archaeological evidence for the native population in the south and east of England; by the time we reach Cheshire, very little is known. On the other hand, Roman military activity was clearly most intense in the north and west. The Romans were therefore clearly dealing with an effective enemy in this area.

The conquest of the West Midlands and Wales (8)

After taking Colchester (Camulodunum), which the expanding anti-Roman tribe of the Catuvellauni had taken over as their capital, the Roman forces fanned out: Legion II *Augusta* advanced into the south-west, Legion XIV north-westwards into the Midlands, and Legion IX due north, while Legion XX was held in reserve at Colchester. By AD 47, the country south-east of a line approximately from the Humber to the Bristol Channel had been occupied.

During the initial stages of the campaign, eleven British kings submitted to the Romans. It is not certain whether these included the rulers of the Cornovii – the tribe in whose territory the site of Chester lay. Some have assumed that they became allies of Rome, but the large campaign bases on their eastern boundaries suggest that they were hostile.

In 47/8, the Romans had to deal with an attack from Wales on some of the tribes who were allied to them. Once the immediate problem had been dealt with the Roman army went on to the offensive. They moved first

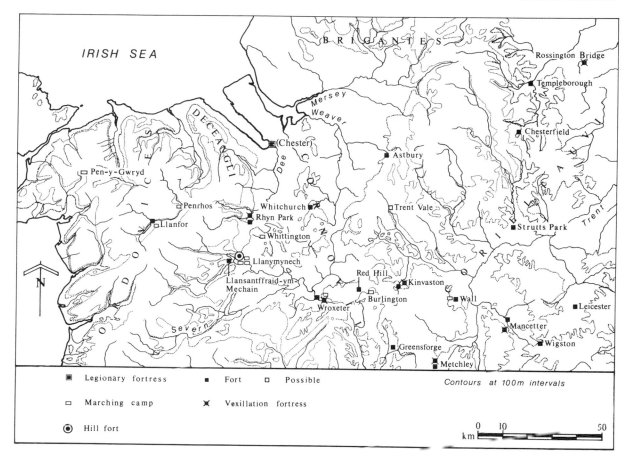

against the tribe of the 'Decangi' (Deceangli) of Flintshire. Operations were then concentrated against the Silures and the Ordovices of South and mid-Wales respectively, who had risen under the leadership of the refugee Catuvellaunian nobleman Caratacus. The site of Caratacus' last stand, with the Ordovices, may have been at the large hillfort near Lanymynech in Shropshire. Although there is no evidence that the Romans camped at or near Chester at this time, they must have become familiar with the area through reconnaissance scouting. To consolidate the position in the Marches an auxiliary fort was now established at Wroxeter, and Legion XX was moved forward to a fortress just outside Gloucester.

The Welsh campaigns continued through the 50s. In the south, Legion XX was moved forward again, to Usk, and in the Marches the auxiliary fort at Wroxeter was replaced by a

8 *Early Roman military sites in the north-western Midlands and North Wales. The temporary camps at Wall, Burlington, Whittington and Penrhos may be evidence for the advance of the Roman army against the Deceangli. Note the multiple siege camps at Llanymynech. 'Vexillation' fortresses accommodated detachments of legions (vexillations), sometimes brigaded together with auxiliaries.*

fortress for Legion XIV. These campaigns culminated in AD 60 in an invasion of the Druidic stronghold of Anglesey, but before the Romans could complete their victory, revolt broke out among the Iceni of East Anglia, under the leadership of their queen, Boudica. Hitherto the tribe had been an ally of Rome and had kept some independence, but when Boudica's husband died the Romans annexed the kingdom in a particularly brutal fashion.

The Anglesey campaign, involving the use of boats to cross the Menai Strait, was thought to have required the use of Chester as a base for both naval and land forces. However, to cross the Strait would only have required very simple craft which could have been built or commandeered on the spot, and at present there is no archaeological evidence for an advance by land along the North Wales coast. By contrast the Dee valley route may already have been used by the Roman army as a line of penetration, and there is a 16ha (40 acres) site at Rhyn Park, near Chirk, close to where the Dee leaves the mountains, which could have been a base for this campaign.

In the mid-50s, the Roman army had become involved in supporting the allied Brigantian queen Cartimandua in a quarrel with her husband Venutius, who was the leader of an anti-Roman faction in the tribe. Venutius eventually took advantage of a civil war in the Roman empire in AD 69 to launch a successful attack on his wife, who had to be rescued by the Romans.

There seems to have been little military activity in Britain between the defeat of Boudica's revolt and the rescue of Cartimandua. The need during these years would have been for reconstruction and consolidation. In addition, Legion XIV was withdrawn later in the decade for service in the east of the Empire; its place at Wroxeter was filled by withdrawing Legion XX from Usk. The military front line in the area under discussion is therefore unlikely to have been advanced; rather, it is probable that it remained on an east–west line a day's march (about 30km (18 miles)) north of Wroxeter, running from Rhyn Park (where a permanent fort overlies the campaign base), through Whitchurch and Stoke-on-Trent. Nevertheless, we may be certain that the Romans maintained diplomatic control of Cheshire and north-eastern Wales.

The seventies and the foundation of Chester

After the fall of Cartimandua, the Romans were virtually compelled to occupy northern England and decided to complete the conquest of Wales. Under three successive governors Brigantia was overrun between 71 and 73, Wales was finally conquered between 74 and 77, and between 78 and 84 Agricola took Roman garrisons as far north as the Tay. It was during these years that the three legionary fortresses were established that were destined to last for the rest of the Roman occupation – at Chester, Caerleon and York.

The main force which overran the Brigantes, led by Legion IX, advanced up the eastern side of the country, while Legion XX advanced from Wroxeter up the western side of the Pennines. There is a large, enigmatic site at Astbury, near Congleton in south-eastern

9 *Lengths of lead water-pipe found north of Eastgate Street in 1899/1900, on the probable site of the commander's house. The inscription reads* IMP VESP VIIII T IMP VII COS GN IVLIO AGRICOLA LEG AVG PR PR *'(Made when) the Emperor Vespasian was consul for the ninth time and Titus, acclaimed imperator, was consul for seventh time, in the governorship of Gnaeus Iulius Agricola' (AD 79).*

Cheshire, which may be a forward base for this campaign.

The main fighting to complete the conquest of Wales in the years 74–7 seems to have been concentrated against the Silures in the south. North-eastern Wales must already have been pacified, since by 74 the Roman authorities had already taken over the Flintshire lead–silver mines, and it is possible that a small fort existed at Chester for a few years before the legionary fortress to supervise the transport of metal from these mines. No buildings of such a fort have been found, but there is a small amount of pottery of this date.

By the mid-70s, therefore, a legionary fortress was needed further to the north-west than Wroxeter in order to control the newly-occupied areas of North Wales and the western Pennines. The many estuaries which penetrated the coasts of North Wales and Lancashire gave the Romans the opportunity to establish supply links between a new legionary base and other garrisons by ship as well as by road. The disadvantages of a base on the Dee were considerable in terms of overland communication between north and south, as it is necessary to backtrack almost 30km (18 miles) to the Runcorn–Warrington area in order to ford the Mersey. On the other hand, the Dee estuary was much easier for shipping. It is not known precisely when work on the fortress began, but it seems from lead water-pipes that date to AD 79 that construction may have been coming to an end in that year (**9**).

The Roman fortress

When it came to selecting an exact site for the new fortress there was little choice. At Chester the river breaks through a north–south sandstone ridge in a narrow gorge. Upstream it meandered through alluvial meadows, while downstream it immediately broadened out into the estuary. Consequently, the site of Chester was the lowest easy crossing point. The fortress was apparently carefully placed on the ridge, where it would enjoy a commanding position

and have the advantage of good drainage (**colour plate 1**).

The Romans called the site Deva 'the goddess', after the native Celtic name for the river, from which also comes the modern 'Dee'. The name is a common one both in Britain and on the continent of Europe. The fact that the fortress was named after a natural feature rather than a man-made one does not prove that there was no native settlement nearby, but rather reflects the nature of native place-names.

Garrisons

The legionary fortress was built by Legion II *Adiutrix Pia Fidelis*. This legion had been raised during the civil war of AD 69 from sailors of the Adriatic fleet based at Ravenna and gained its titles *Pia Fidelis* 'dutiful and faithful' for its support of the new emperor Vespasian. It was sent to Britain to replace Legion XIV *Gemina*, and was initially based at Lincoln. By 88 the legion had been moved again – this time to the Danube frontier to help counter an invasion – and was destined to stay there with its headquarters at Budapest.

The withdrawal from Britain of Legion II *Adiutrix*, and probably of some auxiliaries as well, may well have been behind the decision to abandon the still-incomplete fortress at Inchtuthil on the Tay and begin the withdrawal from the north that eventually halted on the Tyne–Solway line. Inchtuthil had been founded by Agricola to consolidate his conquest of Scotland, and the intended garrison was probably his old legion, the Twentieth (XX). The legion perhaps first returned to its former base at Wroxeter; if so, it soon moved to Chester, and there it was stationed for the rest of the Roman period – or at least until the evidence fails.

The two titles carried by the legion were *Valeria Victrix*, usually abbreviated *V.V.* or *Val. Vic.*, meaning 'Strong and Victorious' (**10**). It did not carry these titles when it arrived in Britain in AD 43, and they were probably awarded for its role in defeating Boudica in

60/1. Early in the third century the legion also carried the title *Antoniniana* after the official family name of the emperor we know as Caracalla (213–22). For a short time in the middle of the third century it was titled *Deciana* after the emperor Trajan Decius. The emblem of the legion was the leaping boar – it is not known when this was adopted, but its ferocity made it a favourite military symbol among the Celts.

Roman military bases of the first to third centuries were intended as bases from which to operate, not as strongholds to withstand sieges. It was normal, therefore, for detachments (often 1000 strong) to be absent from their bases, sometimes for quite long periods. There are many examples of detachments of the legion serving elsewhere, both in Britain and other parts of the empire, but we do not know precisely how long they were absent or how many men were involved. The building of Hadrian's Wall in the 120s was divided between all three British legions, but the largest share of the work fell to the Twentieth. When the next emperor, Antoninus Pius, decided to abandon

Hadrian's Wall and reoccupy southern Scotland in 140, the legion contributed to the invasion force. It also took part in the building of a new frontier work, the Antonine Wall, between the Forth and the Clyde, and in the garrisoning of the newly-won territory. Southern Scotland was evacuated again in the early 160s and the base at Chester seems to have been occupied in strength once more.

The late second and third centuries were a period of increased pressure on the frontiers of the empire and instability within. In 197, again with the other British legions, the Twentieth contributed a force to support the governor of Britain, Clodius Albinus, in his bid for the imperial throne against his rival and the ultimate victor, Septimius Severus. In 208–11 Severus was campaigning in person in Britain to reoccupy southern Scotland again.

The last record of the legion comes from the time of another British pretender to the

10 *Tombstone of Caius Lovesius Cadarus, a soldier of Legion XX V.V. Probably late first century.*

imperial throne, Carausius (287–93). It could have been destroyed, withdrawn or amalgamated at any time in the fourth century; there is no precise information. The coins from Chester – the best indicators of a Roman presence, military or administrative – decline sharply after the 360s.

Throughout the period of the empire, the importance of the legion in its standard form declined in favour of smaller, more specialized units. Finally, towards the end of the third century the emperor Diocletian formally recognized the fragmentation that had been going on and reorganized the legions as units of 1000 men. Moreover, in 197 serving soldiers had been allowed to marry, and it is possible that ultimately their wives were allowed to live within the walls of military bases. However, no clear archaeological evidence has yet been recognized at Chester for a permanent reduction in garrison strength in the fourth century, or for the presence of soldiers' wives and families in the fortress.

Among the military tombstones are a number depicting horsemen. Most of these were probably from among the 120 dispatch riders and scouts kept on the books of all legions. However, one was clearly a Sarmatian cavalryman, from southern Russia. The possibility of an auxiliary unit having been based at Chester should therefore be considered, although no appropriate accommodation for it has yet been found. There is also an early third-century tombstone of a soldier of Legion II *Augusta*, which might hint at a garrison made up of a mixture of units at that time.

Planning

In its essentials Chester fits into the normal pattern of Roman military bases of the mid-first to early third centuries. In outline it was rectangular with rounded corners and on each of the four sides was a gateway giving access to the major streets (**11**). Three of these four streets met at the central crossroads: the fourth side of the crossroads was occupied by the head-

quarters building. Around the periphery and along the main transverse street were the barracks. Those on the western side of the headquarters belonged to the elite troops of the First Cohort. The rest of the space was occupied by the commander's house, houses of the other senior officers, granaries and other stores, workshops, a hospital and baths. Immediately behind the defences were the cook-houses. The fortunes of Chester in later times led to the main Roman streets, and some of the minor ones, surviving in use until the present day.

The high degree of standardization in the layout of Roman fortresses helps to restore the plan of Roman Chester on paper: for example by allowing us to predict which buildings would have occupied as-yet unexcavated areas. Nevertheless, this standardization must not be overemphasized. The size of a 'standard' fortress is often quoted as 20ha (50 acres), but as many deviate from this standard as conform to it. Chester was larger, at 22.5ha (56 acres), and so some of our predictions must be tempered with caution.

The defences

The first defences of the fortress comprised a bank made up of two piles of turf with an infilling of clay and sandstone rubble. Near the base, layers of roughly cut branches were interleaved to increase stability. This rampart measured about 6m (20ft) wide by about 4.5m (15ft) high and was crowned by a wooden palisade. The gateways and interval towers were also made of timber and stood about 7.4m (24ft) high. Just over 1.5m (5ft) in front of the rampart was a ditch, between 3.5m ($11\frac{1}{2}$ft) and 5m ($16\frac{1}{2}$ft) wide and 1.75m (6ft) deep (**colour plate 2**).

About AD 100 the defences were partly reconstructed in stone. In the case of the gateways and towers this meant reconstruction in their entirety. For the rampart, it simply meant adding a stone facing. At the same time as the facing was added, the first ditch was filled with clay in the interests of stability and

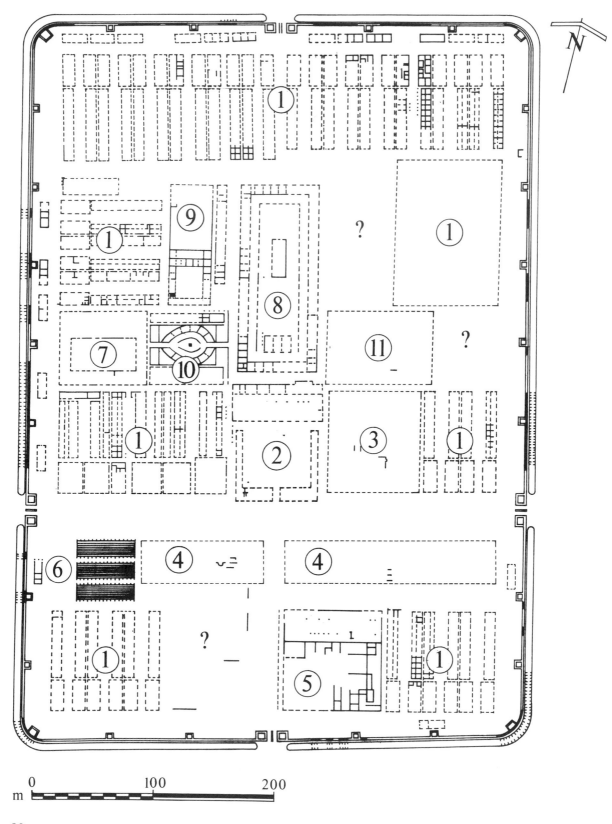

11 *(Left) Plan of the Roman fortress. Not all of the buildings were in use at the same time.*

Key
 1 *Barracks*
 2 *Headquarters building*
 3 *Possible site of commander's residence*
 4 *Probable sites of senior officers' houses*
 5 *Baths*
 6 *Granaries*
 7 *Workshop*
 8 *Possible store-building or hospital*
 9 *Possible store building*
10 *'Elliptical Building'*
11 *Possible site of hospital (if not 8)*

12 *(Below) The north wall of the Roman fortress as it survives today, just east of the Northgate. The curvature of the facing is caused by the settlement of the turf rampart behind.*

a new one was cut further out. This was the same width as the old one, but deeper, measuring about 2.75m (9ft). At the beginning of the third century some of the towers were rebuilt. At the end of that century, or perhaps later, the north wall of the fortress was extensively repaired, as shown by the number of earlier Roman tombstones recovered from this stretch of the walls.

A number of sections of the Roman curtain wall have survived into modern times (**12**); the gateways, on the other hand, although they would have been imposing structures, have now disappeared. Little is known about the fate of the northern gateway but the western and southern gates were probably demolished in the Middle Ages. Parts of the eastern gate survived within the medieval Eastgate until the latter was demolished and replaced by a wider

arch in 1768. An engraving made at the time of the demolition shows that it would have been of a common type with two arches flanked by towers (**13**).

13 *The remains of the Roman gateway revealed when the medieval Eastgate was demolished in 1768.*

Barracks

The barracks, of course, formed the most numerous type of building in the fortress, and their layout reflected the organization of the army. Legions were made up of ten cohorts. Each cohort had six centuries of eighty men, except for the First Cohort, which during the first century AD was double strength. A century was divided into ten groups of eight men, who would form tent-parties when on campaign.

Each barrack accommodated one century, with a separate house for the centurion in command. They were laid out in facing pairs and were generally arranged in groups of six or twelve – that is one or two cohorts. Internally they were divided by a spine wall into pairs of rooms, one pair for each group of men. In front there was a veranda. At one end, separated by a narrow alley were the centurion's quarters. These extended to the full width of the men's quarters and did not have a veranda (**colour plate 3**).

The structural history of the barracks is quite complicated. This is not surprising. Because there were so many of them, it was not possible for them all to be modified or rebuilt at the same time. In broad terms, the full complement of barracks seems to have been constructed in timber at the foundation of the fortress in the late 70s. Between 100 and 120 they underwent various modifications and repairs. By 120, reconstruction in stone – or at least on stone foundations – had begun. Because of the absence of troops away in the north, this operation was suspended, with some buildings incomplete. Reconstruction continued after the abandonment of Scotland in the 160s. There seems to have been a general reconstruction in the early third century and further modification of the barracks in the central area in the fourth century. As we shall see, work on the other buildings in the fortress followed approximately the same pattern.

The headquarters building

The headquarters building was of the standard type, consisting of a large hall with courtyard in front (**14**). The hall had a nave and two side aisles (**15**); behind it lay a range of rooms. Most of these served as offices, but the central one would have been a shrine containing a statue of the emperor and the standards of the legion.

14 *The Roman headquarters building: model in the Grosvenor Museum.*

15 *Column bases and fallen column drums from the main hall of the headquarters building, preserved in the basement of 23 Northgate Street.*

Below it was a cellar (which still survives) serving as the strongroom for the legion's pay-chest. The courtyard was surrounded by ranges of rooms with porticoes on both sides. These rooms may have served as armouries. In the middle of the southern range there would have been a large ceremonial entrance in line with a similar entrance in the hall and the shrine.

33

The headquarters was originally built in timber when the fortress was first founded but we know very little about this first building. Early in the second century it was rebuilt in stone. The new building measured about 73 × 105m (240 × 345ft). It underwent alterations in the middle of the second century, followed by major rebuilding in the early third century and was re-floored in the fourth.

The baths

The baths (**16**) lay in the southern part of the fortress, on the eastern side of Bridge Street. They consisted of an exercise hall, a series of heated rooms and a cold plunge-bath, though far less is known about the fascinating building than we would like. The whole complex was over 80m (260ft) square. The large aisled exercise hall lay on the northern side and was 24m (78ft) wide. The main suite of heated rooms lay to the east (**17**), with the hottest room nearest the stoke-hole at the south-eastern corner. The south-western quarter of the complex was probably an open courtyard containing the cold plunge-bath. Because of its function it was built of stone, brick and concrete from the beginning. Like many buildings in the fortress it seems to have been modified in the early third century.

Other major buildings

The granaries lay on the western side of Bridge Street. They were built in stone in the early second century. Presumably the fortress had timber granaries before then, but no trace of them has yet been recognized. The stone granaries had raised floors, in order to discourage vermin and reduce mould growth by allowing air to circulate, and buttresses to counter the outward pressure of grain stacked against the walls. Calculations suggest that the granaries could have held enough grain to feed the legion for a year. They were re-roofed in the middle of the third century, but had begun to be dismantled by the early fourth century.

In the middle of the fortress, apart from a courtyard-style workshop, were three puzzling buildings. Immediately behind the head-

16 *Reconstruction drawing of the Roman fortress baths* (T.J. Strickland).

TJS.'82

LEG·XX·VV

17 Hypocaust (raised floor) of a heated room south of the exercise hall of the baths, visible from the basement of 41 Northgate Street.

quarters was another courtyard building. When the south-western corner was excavated it was first thought to be the commander's residence, which would normally be expected in this position. However, further discoveries showed it to be a colossal building, about 65 × 157m (215 × 515ft) in plan, with apparently no residential accommodation. Two suggested functions are stores or hospital, although it does not match the fairly standardized plans of buildings fulfilling either of these roles in other fortresses. Two inscriptions by Greek doctors were found in it, but neither of these need have been in their original positions. No medical instruments were found, and the entrances to the rooms were about 3m (10ft) wide – more in keeping with the needs of a store than a hospital. It was built in the 160s, rebuilt in the early third century and modified again and re-floored in the fourth century. Below it were the foundations of an uncompleted stone predecessor, started about the beginning of the second century. Also on its site were traces of timber buildings, presumably put up in the late first century.

To the west of this building lay another, with a small courtyard at the south end and a large enclosure to the north. Again the plan seems to be unique in Roman fortresses. It was built on a vacant plot in the early third century and continued in use with modifications and subdivisions into the fourth. Just to the south lies the strangest building of all: the 'Elliptical Building', so called after the shape of its interior. Construction is thought to have begun in the 70s, at the foundation of the fortress, but it was not completed until the third century. There were further modifications in the fourth century.

18 *The shrine of the goddess Minerva, carved on an outcrop of rock in the Roman quarry in Handbridge.*

Attached to its southern side was a small bathhouse. The plan seems best suited to some sort of social or ceremonial function.

The parade ground and amphitheatre

Two areas outside the fortress walls were reserved for military use. The first consisted of a patch of open ground north of the east gate, apparently surrounded by an earthen bank. This was probably the site of the legionary parade ground.

The second, near the south-eastern corner of the fortress, was the amphitheatre, one of Chester's few visible Roman monuments. Originally built in timber in the 70s, it was rebuilt in stone around 100. It fell into disrepair after 120, when much of the legion was posted north to help build Hadrian's Wall. It was not repaired until after 270, when stone paving slabs were laid in the arena. It was finally abandoned in the fourth century.

The quarries and the shrine of the goddess Minerva

On the south bank of the river Dee are the remains of a large quarry used as a source of building stone for the fortress and, no doubt, some of the major civilian buildings. Excavations have shown that work in the quarry came to an end in the fourth century.

On the eastern face of a small knoll left by the quarrymen is a relief of the goddess Minerva (**18**). As the protector of craftsmen, it was quite appropriate that the quarrymen should seek her assistance. She also faces the bridge over the river Dee and the road south, perhaps as the patron of travellers. She remains there to this day, the only representation of a Classical goddess still in its original position in western Europe.

The civilian settlement (*canabae legionis*)

Legionary fortresses did not exist in isolation: they had far-reaching effects on the native economies, particularly in previously less developed areas. The sudden arrival of 5000–6000 men, together with their dependants, was an influx of foreigners without precedent in Britain.

The population of the civilian settlement must have been very mixed: traders who could supply luxuries not available in the fortress itself and the common-law families of soldiers, who were not permitted to marry before discharge until a late second-century legal reform. Tombstones of retired soldiers show that there was a wide mixture of nationalities from all over the empire.

We know far less in detail about the extra-mural settlement than about the fortress, partly because there has been less excavation; neither was it laid out in the same standardized way, so we cannot make the same sort of predictions about it. Nevertheless, we can begin to build up a general picture.

The growth of the settlement seems to have been rapid: shops and houses were built alongside the main road east almost as soon as the fortress was founded (**19**). Areas to the south and west seem to have been deliberately planned soon afterwards. Within twenty years there was a thriving civil settlement and port.

The location of the ribbon development east of the fortress, between the parade ground to the north and the amphitheatre to the south, suggests that the land was under direct military control. Land here was probably rented or leased from the military authorities. The most intensive period of occupation in this area seems to have ended shortly after 200.

Aqueducts carried water to the fortress from Boughton, 1.5km (1 mile) to the east. Ceramic water-pipes have been found close to Boughton and along the line of Foregate Street, beneath the Roman road. A second line of pipes ran along a more southerly course, probably entering the fortress at its south-eastern corner to supply the intramural bath-house.

South of the fortress, in contrast to the eastern and western sides, a zone about 100m (330ft) wide was kept free of buildings. Beyond that, a number of substantial buildings have been found, including a possible guest-house. The history of this structure parallels that of the buildings within the fortress, supporting its interpretation as an official establishment. The grid-plan of the road layout in this area indicates a more planned development than to the east.

19 *Plan of the Roman fortress and civilian settlement.*

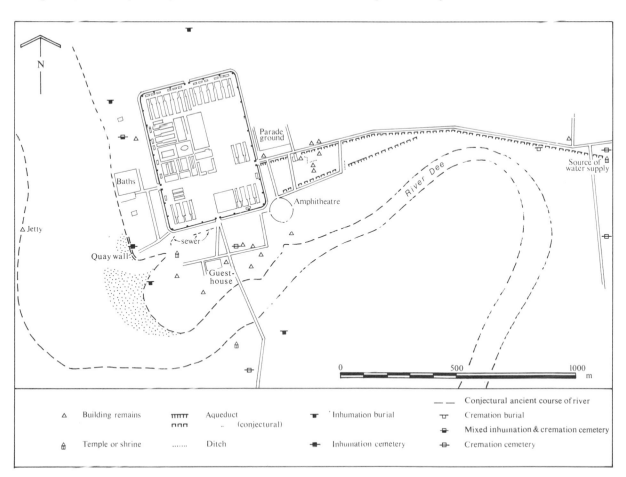

The most substantial building west of the fortress was a bath-house, a building almost certainly owned by the military authorities. Between this and a tidal creek to the south there was dense civilian occupation through to the fourth century. At least one building was a warehouse, while there were also houses with stone foundations and hypocausts, dwellings of some pretensions. North of the bath-house the early second-century occupation was sparser and less affluent, and from the later second century part of the area was a cemetery.

What is now known as the Roodee was at that time a tidal pool, and remains of the Roman quay wall can still be seen beside the racecourse (**20**). Wooden jetties were also discovered when the gasworks were built in the

20 *A section of the Roman quay wall, visible from the Roodee. The medieval City Walls lie directly above.*

nineteenth century. They must have extended well out into the river during the Roman period, and were presumably where ships moored at low tide.

North of the fortress no Roman buildings have been discovered, although there may have been scattered settlement, less substantial than elsewhere.

Legal status of the civilian settlement
It was normal for *canabae* ('wine-booths') to grow up outside legionary fortresses, and the legionary commander would control their siting. Their status was that of *vicus*, which was

the lowest grade of independent settlement.

There is no firm indication of urban function for the civilian settlement. This contrasts strongly with York, where it had become a chartered town by the time of Severus' death there in 211. There are no truly public buildings; the guest-house was a government establishment, and the extramural bath-house was a normal feature of civilian settlements. On the other hand, with reductions in the size of legions during the third century, it is possible that urban functions took place inside the walls and that military buildings were turned over to civilian use.

Cemeteries

Only one cemetery at Chester is known in detail, that in the Infirmary Field, to the west of the fortress. The cemetery was laid out in rows, with graves aligned roughly north–south or east–west. The burials range from cremations in pits, through simple graves, tile-lined cists to rubble and concrete tombs – types known from other military sites in Britain. The remains of both sexes were found, as well as juveniles, so this was not a purely military cemetery

Burials have been found elsewhere. There are reports of burials north of the fortress, and in 1984 the lead lining of a coffin was found in the area. There seems to have been a cemetery on the edge of the Roodee, above the quay wall, but it is poorly recorded. To the south, in the vicinity of St Olave's Street, a few early cremations have been found, with more across the river Dee in Handbridge, where a cemetery lined the road south.

There are also burials from Boughton, an area with little evidence for settlement. These burials were near the springs which supplied the fortress with water and which were believed to have sacred properties.

The countryside and *prata legionis*

The army must have transformed the countryside. Roads were constructed, largely for the movement of troops and state officials, but were also available for use by the civilian population. An area was requisitioned by the army for use as farmland and the supply of other raw materials. The *prata legionis* ('meadows of the legion') may have covered an area in excess of 500 sq.km (190 sq.miles), and could have included all the Wirral peninsula as well as part of the West Cheshire plain (**21**).

The arrival of Roman administration also brought about fundamental changes in the local economy. Farmers now had to produce a surplus for taxation, although this is unlikely to have placed a strain on late pre-Roman Iron Age farming methods which were already capable of producing surpluses. Farmers closer to the fortress may have suffered more, with direct requisitioning and control of their lands by the military.

Although rural settlement around Chester is poorly understood, occupation debris is found throughout western Cheshire. Some derives from small rural settlements, either individual farmsteads or hamlets, while scatters of pottery and tile at places such as Kelsall and Frodsham point to the existence of larger settlements with substantial buildings.

The discovery of a villa with stone foundations at Eaton-by-Tarporley, hints of a stone building with painted wall plaster at Tattenhall and a hypocaust at Crewe Hall, Farndon, show that some local people had Romanized tastes. It is unlikely that all such buildings were the homes of retired soldiers, although the discovery of military diplomas (discharge certificates) such as the one from Malpas, suggests that veterans did occasionally retire to the country.

Most of the evidence for substantial buildings lies outside the area thought to have been the *prata legionis*. Indeed, the only evidence west of the river Gowy and in Wirral consists of the possible building at Tattenhall and a recently-discovered site near Irby. These may have been farms run under military licence. There are no concentrations of material suggestive of small-scale or nucleated settlements as are found outside this area, and this strengthens the case for its special status. In the case of Irby occupation seems to have begun during the third century, a time when the former *prata legionis* may have reverted to civilian control.

Heronbridge and Saltney

Excavations at Heronbridge have uncovered substantial Roman buildings which were occupied throughout the Roman period. It was once thought that the settlement grew up around a dock, where pottery and tiles brought downstream from Holt were off-loaded for transport by road to Chester. However, the 'dock' has been shown to be a culverted stream which may not even be Roman.

The form of the settlement – ribbon development along Watling Street – suggests natural growth. Where side streets occur they do not give the impression of the regular grid pattern of planned settlements. Other legionary fortresses in western Europe have similar satellite settlements. These are thought to have been

21 *Map of Cheshire and Flintshire in Roman times, showing settlements, the* prata legionis, *kilns and quarries.*

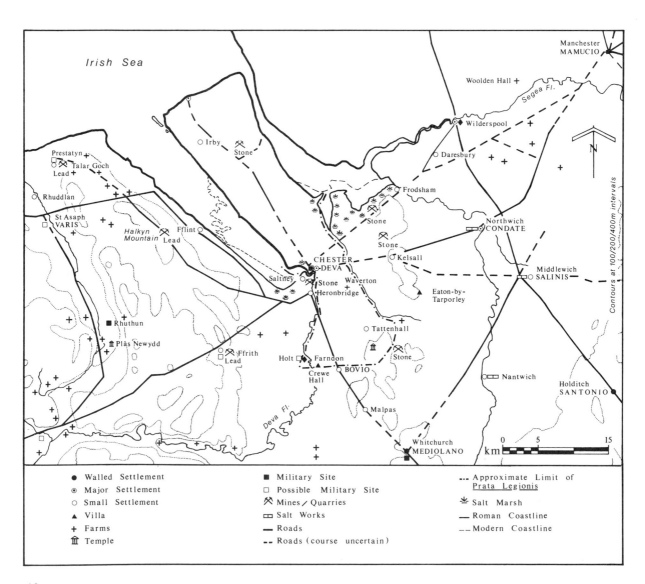

inhabited by natives, while the *canabae* were largely settled by foreigners, often with close personal ties to the garrison. The *canabae* stood on ground owned by the legion; the satellite settlements stood on privately-owned ground.

North-west of Heronbridge at Saltney another settlement was discovered during the building of a housing estate at the Lache in the 1920s. Little is known about it. It seems to have been occupied throughout the Roman period. The few remains found point to a less dense form of settlement than at Heronbridge, possibly a farming and fishing community.

Roman inscriptions from Chester

Most Romano-British sites of any size have produced the occasional tombstone or inscription. Yet bearing in mind the numbers of people who lived in these settlements and the length of time they were occupied, the number of surviving inscriptions is very small indeed. Chester, however, is an exception. The city has produced the largest number of Roman inscriptions from a single site anywhere in Britain, and their discovery in Victorian times was to make a considerable impact on the study of Roman Britain and the Roman army.

During repairs to the northern section of the City Walls in 1883 the City Surveyor began to find pieces of sculptured and inscribed stones, and soon realized that they were Roman. In the course of the following nine years the North Wall was systematically investigated, and by the end of 1892 over 200 complete or fragmentary inscriptions and sculptures had been recovered.

It was obvious that Roman stones had been reused as building blocks to strengthen the walls at some time in the distant past. Fortunately, their new function had protected them from the worst ravages of weather and time. Many of them, however, bore the scars from their conversion to their new use: tombstones had been cut in half to make them into a more manageable size, and the high relief of sculptures had been crudely chiselled away in

order to make sure that the stone would lie flat.

A great number of the stones are clearly tombstones. Some take the form of a plain inscription, while others are a more elaborate type with the wording topped by a sculptured relief showing the dead person. Many of the other sculptured figures and panels can be shown to have a connection with death or beliefs about the afterlife and it seems reasonably certain that all of the stones had been removed from one of the cemeteries which lay outside the Roman fortress walls. The sculptures and panels must have been stripped from the type of elaborate stone vault or funeral monument known from other Roman sites to have been set up by the wealthier members of the community. It is not likely that they would have been moved very far; the nearest known cemetery lay on the north-western side of the fortress, under the Royal Infirmary.

Since Chester was primarily a legionary base it is not surprising that most of the tombstones commemorate soldiers. There are thirteen stones of men of Legion II *Adiutrix* and the vast majority of the remaining military tombstones are of men of Legion XX *Valeria Victrix*. The sheer number of stones means that most ranks in the legion are represented at least once, from the ordinary soldier up to the commander.

The stones range in date from the 70s until the early third century. It is somewhat surprising that most of them seem to date to the second century, a period when other evidence suggests that the fortress was very lightly occupied.

The inscriptions give a remarkably vivid impression of the cosmopolitan population of a military site during the first and second centuries. They commemorate soldiers from as far away as Spain, France, Italy and Slovenia; some are even from European and Asian Turkey. The quality of workmanship varies from stone to stone, but is generally poorer than might be expected from legionary craftsmen. Some of the later pieces, such as the tombstone of the centurion Marcus Aurelius Nepos and his wife, are remarkably crude (**22**).

Civilians are also well represented in the collection, and their tombstones give a hint of the size and prosperity of the *canabae* outside the fortress walls. One is in memory of Flavius Callimorphus, aged forty-two, and his son Serapion, who died when he was three years and six months old. It seems likely that Callimorphus was a Greek trader who had settled in Chester with his family. As on several other stones, his memorial shows the dead couple reclining on a couch and enjoying a meal, a motif which seems to have referred to the prospect of happiness after death (**23**).

Another 'funeral banquet' scene appears on the elegant tombstone of Curatia Dinysia, a lady with a Greek name who died at the age of forty (**24**). Except for the quality of the stone itself there is nothing to indicate what sort of person she was or why she was living in Chester. She may have been a rich civilian, perhaps a merchant's daughter, or a relative of one of the senior officers in the fortress.

The sculptured fragments which were recovered with the tombstones are full of references to the legends of the classical Mediterranean, such as Hercules rescuing Hesione from a sea monster, or Actaeon being torn to pieces by his hounds. The style of the carving is again rather primitive, although this may not have been so apparent in Roman times when the surface of the stone would have been finished with a coat of thin plaster and paint. The presence of these sculptures shows a knowledge of classical civilization which is quite surprising for the north-western frontier of the Roman world; we are left to guess at the quality and size of the monuments which they once adorned.

Pottery supply to Roman Chester (25)

The establishment of military garrisons and the growth of towns soon stimulated the growth of pottery industries in Roman Britain. Many of the types of vessels used by the Romans were already made by the tribes of southern and eastern England, the main exceptions being

22 *Early third-century tombstone of the centurion Marcus Aurelius Nepos and his wife.*

flagons and *mortaria* (large, grit-studded mixing bowls), which were initially imported. Finer wares continued to be imported through much of the Roman period.

In the north and west of Britain the native pottery was of poor quality. As the Roman army occupied these areas, workshops were set up to produce pottery specifically for military use. It might be expected that such workshops would have been set up to serve the fortress at Chester. However, as we shall see below, those that are known, at Holt, seem to have been established at the very end of the first century, in response to a different stimulus.

23 *'Theseus set up this tombstone to his brother Flavius Callimorphus and his son Serapion'. The names are Greek.*

24 *The best preserved of all the Chester tombstones, dedicated to Curatia Di(o)nysia, who died at the age of 40.*

Most of the late first-century pottery found in Chester comprised vessels in a grey fabric which were probably made locally. The forms were similar to those used in the Rhineland, where most of the army of Britain had been based before the invasion. This suggests that they were manufactured by soldiers or camp-followers from that area. The army's demand for certain types of vessels such as *mortaria* stimulated their production in Britain. The main source of this type of vessel in the first century was the St Albans area. The fine tableware found at Chester during this period was predominantly the glossy red 'samian' which originated in South Gaul.

For the first twenty or so years of the second century, almost all of the pottery – fine and coarse – used by the Chester garrison was produced at the works-depot at Holt. Once pottery production ceased there in the 120s, Legion XX *V.V.* had to rely on civilian suppliers. This change also coincided with one in the source of samian in Central Gaul.

From the 120s onwards most coarse pottery vessels at Chester were in the form of 'black-burnished' ware. This ware was made in Dorset and derived from the local pre-Roman Iron Age pottery. It came to dominate both military

25 *Roman pottery from Chester:* (left to right) *Nene Valley beaker; South Spanish amphora for fish sauce; mid-first century Lyon ware beaker; black-burnished ware dish; St Albans area* mortarium; *samian cup and dish; Severn Valley ware storage jar*

and civilian markets throughout all but eastern Britain. An offshoot of the industry was established near Doncaster. The major civilian pottery industry in the north-west during the second century was at Wilderspool, near Warrington. The main products from these kilns to reach Chester were *mortaria* and beakers. Other Cheshire pottery industries are known at Northwich and in Chester itself, in the eastern extramural settlement.

Pottery from the Severn Valley, which had a small share of the market in Chester while the Holt kilns were still in production, began to appear in significant quantities during the mid-second and third centuries. The forms included storage jars, bowls and tankards.

About the end of the second century the Wilderspool kilns ceased production. This affected the supply of *mortaria*, which from now

on largely came from kilns at Hartshill and Mancetter in Warwickshire. The supply of Central Gaulish samian also came to an end and was only partly replaced by East Gaulish products. Fine ware – principally beakers – began to reach Chester from the Nene Valley near Peterborough and from the Moselle. The supply of the former continued until the fourth century, the latter until the barbarian invasions across the Rhine frontier in the middle of the third century. These invasions also put an end to the East Gaulish samian industry and prompted the production of imitation samian forms at kilns in Oxfordshire. These kilns also became an additional source for *mortaria*.

In the mid-fourth century black-burnished ware ceased to be widely distributed, possibly because the seaways by which it was transported had become unsafe. Its place in Chester was taken by vessels in a coarse shelly fabric, probably made in the East Midlands. A further reduction in the supply of pottery to Chester was brought about by the collapse of the production centres in the Nene Valley and Oxfordshire during the second half of the century. By the early fifth century it appears that in Chester, as in many other places, pottery had virtually gone out of use.

Amphorae served as containers for the transport of bulk commodities from the Mediterranean, such as olive oil, wine and fish sauces. A wide variety of forms occur in Chester, the most common being the globular amphora from southern Spain which contained olive oil. Rare and unusual forms also occur, such as the 'carrot' amphora, thought to have held dates. In the Late Roman period amphorae came from North Africa and the eastern Mediterranean.

Holt: the works-depot of Legion XX V.V.

Towards the end of the first century AD kilns were established near the modern village of Holt, about 12km (7^1/$_2$ miles) south of Chester, to supply building materials and pottery to the legionary fortress and other military installations in the area. Much of the fortress at Chester was being rebuilt at this time in a more permanent fashion and this created a large demand for ceramic building materials.

The depot covered an area of about 8ha (20 acres) (**26**). The industrial structures included two groups of workshops, one with a heated drying room. There was also an unusually large, double-flue pottery kiln and a main plant of eight kilns. Unfortunately, it is not clear which kilns were used for firing pottery and which for tiles.

The domestic structures comprised a rectangular, walled compound containing the workmen's quarters. These consisted of three barrack blocks, latrines and store buildings. North-east of the compound was a baths building and a small house, probably occupied by the officer-in-charge.

Because the site was excavated early in the twentieth century, when archaeological techniques were still undeveloped, only general comments can be made about the history of

the site and the dating of the finds. We think that pottery production came to an end about AD 125/30, when the absence of detachments of Legion XX *V.V.* on the northern frontier led to reduced demand. Thereafter, local garrisons relied on civilian manufacturers for their pottery. Tile manufacture, however, continued until at least the early third century, although output would have fluctuated according to the amount of building work in progress.

Roofing tiles were the main products of the kilns, although brick and tile for other building purposes were also made, together with more unusual products, such as tubes for vaulting, antefixes (decorative triangular tiles to adorn the ends of roof ridges) and socketed water-pipes.

Pottery was also produced in considerable quantities in a range of common forms, including flagons, jugs, beakers, jars, cups, bowls, dishes and *mortaria* (**27**). Many of the vessels were made in a distinctive coarse orange fabric

26 *Plan of the Roman works-depot at Holt.*

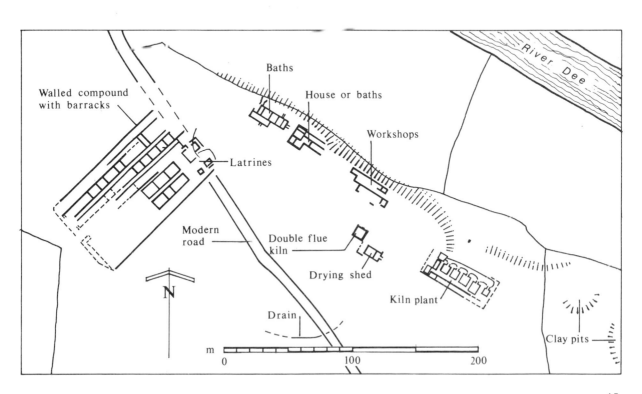

27 *Selection of pottery and building materials made at Holt: flagon, jar, storage jar and bowl; flat roof tile* (tegula), *antefix embossed with the name of the legion and the charging boar, box tile from heating system and vaulting tube.*

which was sometimes coated with a white slip. A range of unusual forms was also produced. Many of these imitated glass, metal and samian vessels and had red-slipped or burnished surfaces. Other decorative techniques included slip-painting, mica-dusting and lead-glazing. A very fine white pottery, known as 'eggshell' ware, was also made, usually in the form of small, conical cups. These exotic wares and some of the manufacturing techniques suggest an eastern Mediterranean influence.

We know very little about the people who worked at Holt. The complex is essentially military in its layout, and there is little doubt that the men who built the structures were legionaries. It is probable that legionaries also produced most of the building materials and pottery, much of which is purely functional in character. The exotic wares, however, could have been made by slaves from the eastern Mediterranean.

The reason why the Holt depot was not set up until the end of the first century is not fully understood. Certainly, there would have been an increased need for tile and brick then. On the other hand, large quantities of serviceable pottery would have been needed from the time that the fortress was established. It may be significant that the exotic forms of pottery produced at Holt were made at a time when there appears to have been a marked decline in imports of samian vessels from France. One motive behind pottery production at Holt, therefore, may have been import substitution. Similar ranges of pottery and building materials were also produced at the other permanent legionary fortresses at Caerleon and York, which were being rebuilt at about the same time. Presumably this reflects a general military quartermastering policy. The works depots at which they were made were probably similar to the one at Holt, but they have not yet been found.

The Flintshire lead mines in the Roman period

For writers of the Roman period, metals were among the noteworthy products of Britain. With the exception of iron, which occurs in the East Midlands and the south-east, the main metal deposits lie in the mountainous areas of western and northern Britain. Within the area for which the Chester garrison was responsible were the copper mines on the Great Orme at Llandudno, on the North Wales coast, as well as on Anglesey, and lead–silver mines in Flintshire. The other main lead–silver mining areas in Roman Britain were in Somerset (the Mendips), Derbyshire, Shropshire and Yorkshire.

Lead was a by-product of the search for silver, as the two metals occurs in the same ore (galena). However, it was also needed for its own sake, to make water-pipes and sheets for use in baths and other types of building work, coffin linings and so on. The Flintshire ores were second only to those of the Mendips for their silver content.

In the Roman empire, mines were a state monopoly, as the supply of precious metals was vital to the maintenance of the gold and silver coinage. They were worked either directly or were leased to private contractors, who paid half of the metal extracted to the imperial treasury. Slaves and criminals usually provided the workforce. Troops were often stationed in mining areas to maintain security, and were also sometimes used to start up production.

All the mining areas in Britain were under direct government control at some time. However, private contractors appeared initially in Flintshire and were common in Derbyshire. It seems likely that the mines which produced the most silver would have been run directly by the government, while others might be leased.

For transport in bulk, the lead was cast into ingots. Most of the information about the lead–silver mining industry in Britain comes from examples of these ingots, apparently lost or abandoned in transit. The ingots were oblong with splayed sides and ends and mostly weighed between 60 and 90kg (130 and 200lb).

The earliest ingot from the Flintshire field was produced by a lessee. It has the cast inscription C NIPI ASCANI 'property of Caius Nipius Ascanius' and dates to the 60s, as the name of the same man appears stamped on an ingot from the Mendips with a cast inscription of Nero, datable to AD 60. It seems that Ascanius

28 *Lead ingot found beneath the Roodee in 1886. The inscription on the top reads 'IMP. VESP. AVG. V. T. IMP. III [CO]S.'; that on the side 'DECANGL' (Cast when) the Emperor Vespasian was consul for the fifth time and Titus, acclaimed imperator, was consul for the third time. Deceanglian (lead)' (AD 74).*

was both trading in ingots produced under government control in the Mendips and running his own mines in Flintshire. At this time Flintshire was probably still outside the limits of Roman military occupation. However, the Romans had already fought one campaign there, in 48, and the area was pacified.

The other ingots from Flintshire have cast imperial inscriptions, of Vespasian and Domitian, showing that the mines came under direct government control. The two earliest belong to 74, the year in which the final conquest of Wales began. Both of these ingots come from Chester: one from the Roodee (**28**), together with what could have been the remains of a jetty; the other from 2km ($1^1/_4$ miles) east of the city. It is likely that neither of these ingots were destined for Chester itself, but were bound further afield. Two more ingots, again with inscriptions of Vespasian and datable to 76, have been found by the side of Watling Street near Tamworth. A group of twenty ingots from Flintshire was found on the banks of the Mersey at Runcorn, where they had again presumably been lost during trans-shipment. Some were dated to 76, others to the reign of Domitian (81–96).

The lead mining area in Flintshire stretched for 35km (22 miles) from Meliden, near Prestatyn on the North Wales coast, to Ffrith, northwest of Wrexham, in the south. Settlements thought to be associated with the industry have been found at Prestatyn and Ffrith, and at the latter there may also have been a fort. A building at Pentre Ffwrndan ('Village of the Furnaces'), on the banks of the Dee estuary, may have been used for the administration of the mines. The main mining field was on the north-eastern scarp of Halkyn Mountain, overlooking Flint. Stamped tiles of Legion XX *V.V.* have been found at Pentre, Prestatyn and Ffrith, pointing to some sort of military involvement or supervision (**21**).

There are no stamped ingots later than the reign of Domitian to indicate how long the Flintshire industry went on, although this may be just the chance of discovery: the building at Pentre continued in use until the mid-third century. If control of the industry had passed to private contractors, there could have been a gradual change to smaller or uninscribed ingots. Nevertheless, it may be that the last thirty years of the first century were indeed the heyday of the industry. Large quantities of lead would have been needed for the massive fort-building programme that followed the conquest of Wales and northern Britain and in the upsurge in urbanization in the south. There was also an increase in the minting of silver coins under Vespasian which would have called for increased output from the mines. By the third century it is likely that much lead was being reused.

However, this was not the end of the story for the Flintshire lead industry. The deposits were exploited again in the Middle Ages and from the seventeenth century until the twentieth, and, as we shall see, are recorded among the exports from the port of Chester.

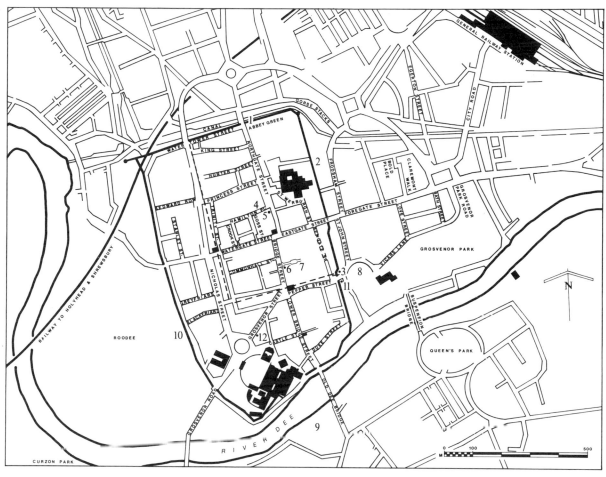

29 *Map of present-day Chester showing the location of visible Roman remains.*

1 *Roman masonry in the North Wall, east of the Northgate*
2 *Lower courses of Roman fortress wall in front of East Wall*
3 *South-East Angle Tower*
4 *Headquarters strongroom in Hamilton Place*
5 *Columns and column bases from main hall of headquarters building in the cellar of 23 Northgate Street*
6 *Hypocaust of bath house in the cellar of 41 Bridge Street*
7 *Mosaic of bath house in cellar of 18 St Michael's Row*
8 *Amphitheatre*
9 *Shrine of Minerva*
10 *Quay wall (visible from race course)*
11 *'Roman Gardens' – architectural fragments from various buildings, especially the bath-house*
12 *Grosvenor Museum displays*
(To see remains in commercial premises, please ask the management and avoid busy times.)

4

Dark Age and Saxon Chester

Sources of evidence

The early fifth century saw the collapse of the Roman empire in the west. Coinage no longer reached Britain after AD 402, and within thirty years manufacturing industries had vanished. The economy and political organization returned to a prehistoric state. In dealing with the fifth and sixth centuries archaeology is at its most tentative; only in recent years have we begun to develop techniques by which we can find what is termed 'Sub-Roman' archaeology, the material evidence of Rome's former citizens. The remains of the later Saxon period are more easily recovered, but, in Chester at least, are still far less substantial than those of the Roman or medieval periods.

Reliable contemporary written histories for the fifth to seventh centuries do not exist. The Venerable Bede is the only true historian of the period, but for periods before his own lifetime (c. 685–735) his work is selective. The *Anglo-Saxon Chronicle* was first compiled at the end of the ninth century and updated in different versions over the next three centuries. It is a dependable and detailed source for the later Saxon period, but it is not trustworthy before the ninth century.

Historical summary

Despite the limitations of our information, it has become possible to construct a general outline of the history of the so-called 'Dark Ages'. The fifth century appears to have been a period of increasing political fragmentation. In 410 the Roman emperor Honorius, under great pressure closer to home, abandoned responsibility for the defence of Britain to the local civil authorities. In the south and east these gradually broke up into smaller units, based on the estates of powerful landowners. In the north and west, where Romanization had never been strong and civilian authorities were rare, political control fell into the hands of local war-lords. Fragmentation increased throughout the fifth century with the arrival of small numbers of immigrants from northern Europe and the emergence of tiny states covering only a few square kilometres.

Only with the growth of the Anglo-Saxon kingdoms in the sixth and particularly seventh centuries did these tiny states begin to disappear, although some groups in remote areas retained a degree of independence until the eleventh century. Two large kingdoms came into prominence during the seventh century: Northumbria in the north of England and Mercia in the Midlands (**30**), with their common boundary ultimately settling on the Mersey (the 'frontier river' in Old English). During the ninth century Wessex, in the south-west, also emerged as a political force.

During the second half of the ninth century, Danish armies seized Northumbria and the eastern part of Mercia, while Norse raiders dominated the Irish Sea. Wessex thus became the sole English power to survive and lead the

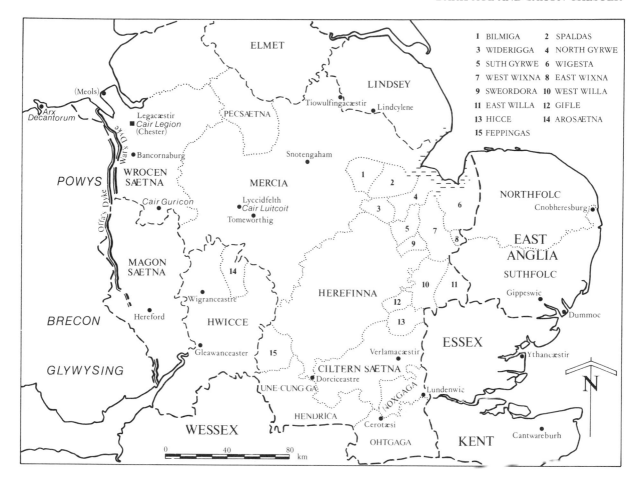

The following labels appear on the map:

1 BILMIGA 2 SPALDAS
3 WIDERIGGA 4 NORTH GYRWE
5 SUTH GYRWE 6 WIGESTA
7 WEST WIXNA 8 EAST WIXNA
9 SWEORDORA 10 WEST WILLA
11 EAST WILLA 12 GIFLE
13 HICCE 14 AROSÆTNA
15 FEPPINGAS

30 *Map showing the peoples of Mercia.*

reconquest. In the early years of the tenth century eastern Mercia was gradually recovered, and in 920 Northumbria acknowledged the overlordship of the English King Edward. Chester's strategic position continued to ensure that it featured in many key events of these centuries.

Sub-Roman Chester

Although there is no archaeological evidence for it, Christianity almost certainly reached Chester during the Roman period. The sixth-century monk Gildas mentions the martyrs Aaron and Julius, citizens of a place called *Legionum Urbs* ('the City of the Legions'). Their home is usually thought to have been Caerleon in South Wales, but the name could equally well refer to Chester. Gildas has traditionally been connected with the monastery of Bangor-is-Coed near Chester, so it may be that he used local stories about the city's earliest martyrs.

The tenth-century Welsh Annals mention a synod at '*Urbs Legion*', which they date to around 603. This meeting was probably the same as Saint Augustine's second conference with the British clergy described by Bede. He does not mention where it took place, but says that seven British bishops and many learned men from Bangor-is-Coed attended. Chester seems the most likely place for this meeting. At this time, Chester may have lain within the Welsh kingdom of Powys, and may even have been the capital of part of it.

The Battle of Chester

Bede follows his account of St Augustine's second synod with the report of a battle at

51

Chester, in which Aethelfrith, king of Bernicia, defeated Brochwel, ex-king of Powys. The same battle is also referred to in the Welsh Annals and in the Irish Annals of Tigernach. The date implied by these Annals is 616.

Bernicia was a kingdom on the coast of Northumberland. It is not known precisely what Aethelfrith was doing at Chester, but he had overrun the kingdom of Deira, based at York, about 605 (thus forming the kingdom of Northumbria) and may have been attempting to extend his power to the south-west when he came into conflict with the kingdom of Powys. However, his campaign had no lasting impact and Chester was not brought into the Northumbrian realm.

Mercian Chester (seventh century to 907)

Chester eventually fell under Saxon control during the seventh-century expansion of Merica. The Mercian kings Penda (c. 634–55), Wulfhere (657–75) and Aethelred I (675–704) pursued vigorous military campaigns against their neighbours, whether fellow-Saxons or Welsh. The first dated event in the history of Mercian Chester was the founding of St John's Church outside the Roman fortress, said by the Annals of St Werburgh's to have occurred in 689.

In the eighth century the remarkable King Offa (754–96) constructed a massive defensive work on the western borders of his kingdom. He built the dyke which still bears his name from Chepstow in the south to Treuddyn in the north. At a later date, perhaps in the ninth century, another dyke – Wat's Dyke – was built in the north, slightly east of Offa's Dyke. It is presumably associated with the campaigns waged by the Mercian kings in North Wales in the first twenty years of the ninth century.

In 875 the inhabitants of Hanbury in Staffordshire are said to have fled to Chester during the Viking invasions which had driven out the Mercian King Burhred (852–73/4). They brought with them the relics of St Werburgh, a Mercian princess, which they

deposited in a long-established church of Saints Peter and Paul, subsequently re-dedicated to St Werburgh. Another version of the story places these events slightly later, in connection with the foundation of the burh.

Chester in the tenth century

In 893/4 a Danish army marched from Essex up the borderland between the Danes and the Saxons and passed the winter at Chester in the old Roman fortress. In 902 the Norsemen were temporarily ejected from Dublin. Soon afterwards, a group under an adventurer called Ingimund settled on the Wirral and tried unsuccessfully to seize Chester. In response to this threat, Aethelflaed, daughter of King Alfred and wife of Aethelred, ealdorman of Mercia, established a burh at Chester in 907. A burh was a stronghold in which the local population could seek refuge from the Vikings. A series of regularly-spaced burhs had already been successfully used by King Alfred in Wessex and was extended by his successors. Cheshire was created as an administrative area to support the burh.

In the years that followed, Danish-held areas were gradually reconquered. Four small burhs were established to guard the Mersey frontier against attacks from Northumbria and the Irish Sea: Eddisbury and Runcorn were built in 914 and 915, and Thelwall and Manchester in 919. In the 920s Lancashire between the Ribble and the Mersey was transferred from Northumbria to the English kingdom and regarded as an appendage of Cheshire. In 921 English power in North Wales was reasserted by the establishment of a burh at Cledemutha (Rhuddlan).

In 916 the Norse returned to Dublin, and a great age of Irish Sea trade soon began. Chester grew rapidly and enjoyed great prosperity as one of the main centres of this trade. Under King Athelstan (924–39) it was the most prolific mint in England, and it also developed as a centre of administration. In 973 British and Viking princes of the north-west demonstrated their submission to the Saxon King Edgar by rowing him up the river Dee to St John's Church. However, in 980 Cheshire suffered a Viking raid and a period of economic decline followed. The English also lost parts of north-eastern Wales which they had previously controlled.

The archaeology of sub-Roman and Mercian Chester

The archaeology of the five centuries following the end of Roman rule at Chester is very obscure. There have been few finds or structures which can be dated to this period, and we cannot confirm or deny the accuracy of the documentary sources.

Amphora sherds of possible fifth- and sixth-century date have been found inside the fortress. These amphorae are of a ribbed form which occurs on a small number of high-status sub-Roman sites in the west and they support the suggestion that Chester became the base for a British war-lord or king, probably of the northern part of the kingdom of Powys.

The so-called 'dark earth' found on many Romano-British sites following the end of the Roman period occurs occasionally at Chester. Recent work suggests that these deposits are a product of root and worm activity. Other deposits which formed between the fourth and

tenth centuries are equally hard to interpret. At a site excavated in Lower Bridge Street in 1991, for instance, after a rough cobbled surface was laid in the fourth century two deposits containing only second-century material formed. These were then sealed by a cultivation deposit cut by a tenth-century pit.

Another excavation in Lower Bridge Street produced sherds of a Carolingian vessel of eighth- or ninth-century date, a ninth-century silver brooch (**31**) and structures dated to the second half of that century.

There is therefore very little direct evidence to tell us what Chester looked like during these centuries. We can infer that the Roman buildings would gradually have become increasingly derelict. Obviously the more substantial, stone structures like the defences, headquarters building and baths would have survived fairly well, whereas half-timbered buildings like the barracks would soon have disappeared. For example, the siege which the Danes withstood in the city at the end of the ninth century shows that the Roman defences were still usable at that time. St Peter's Church,

31 *Silver disc brooch with a pattern in the form of an expanded-arm cross, about 850–900. Found during excavations in Lower Bridge Street.*

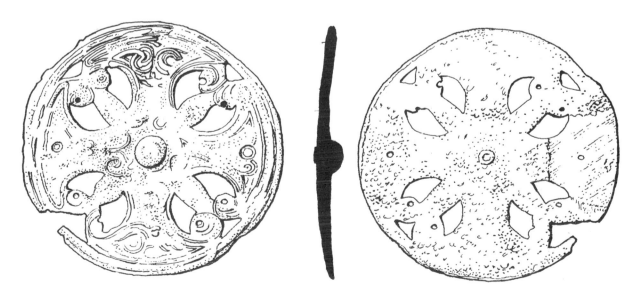

which stands at the Cross on the south-eastern corner of the headquarters building, is usually said to be a tenth-century foundation. However, it is possible that there was already a church on the site: it is precisely here that we would expect to find a late Roman centre of Christianity, and the basilica of the headquarters building may have housed the synod mentioned by Bede.

The fact that major elements of the fortress survived to be taken over when Chester began to grow again in the tenth century suggests that occupation during the 'Dark Ages' had not been intensive enough to obliterate them and impose new patterns. The churches may well have been built of stone, which would have been robbed from Roman buildings, but other buildings would have been of timber.

Nevertheless, the attack by Norse refugees from Ireland which led to the foundation of the burh in 907 was supposedly prompted by the wealth of the city. It may be that the main Mercian settlement lay outside the Roman walls, along Lower Bridge Street and possibly around St John's Church.

The countryside

There are remarkable hints of sub-Roman continuity outside Chester. The evidence comes from place-names, church dedications and the landscape. South of Chester is the village of Eccleston. Its name contains an Old Welsh word *egles, derived from Latin *ecclesia*, 'church'. This element was borrowed by the English speakers who coined the name, probably in the seventh century. There was Saxon masonry in the medieval church, demolished in the nineteenth century, which stood in an oval churchyard. Churchyards of this shape occur in the west of Britain and are associated with Celtic Christianity.

Other villages near Chester also had oval churchyards like that at Eccleston: Great Barrow, Tarvin (which is a British place-name), Farndon (an Anglo-Saxon royal estate), Dodleston and possibly Waverton and Pulford. At Tattenhall the church was dedicated to St Alban, while at Tarporley one was dedicated to St Helen. Dedications to these Roman saints are unusual and are frequently early.

Another community of Christians is recorded in the English name Christleton. The church here again stands in an oval enclosure, so the community was probably British. That their identity was seen as a mark of sufficient distinction to incorporate it into a new place-name suggests that it was coined before the conversion of the majority of the Anglo-Saxon population.

The places with evidence for sub-Roman Christianity are concentrated in a very restricted area. It is possible that they were part of a territory with strong Christian associations administered from Chester. By plotting their distribution it may be possible to suggest the limits of this small state or early Christian bishopric (**32**).

Further afield, a pilgrim's flask has been found at Meols (**33**). It came from the shrine of St Menas, an Egyptian saint whose shrine in Alexandria was destroyed in the seventh century. Its form is of sixth- or seventh-century type, and may attest to trade continuing here. There is also a large collection of sub-Roman metalwork from the site.

The archaeology of Late Saxon Chester

A major burst of activity in and around the old fortress occurred after the foundation of the burh (**34**). This dramatic expansion was presumably accompanied by a corresponding increase in the population, with wider-ranging trade links and a greater variety of occupations. It is noteworthy, however, that after the initial construction there seems to have been little further expansion or development.

Tenth- and eleventh-century occupation is found widely across the site of the old Roman fortress, except in its north-western corner. Intensive occupation has also been found to the south, along Lower Bridge Street. This area

32 (*Right*) *Possible early ecclesiastical enclave around Chester.*

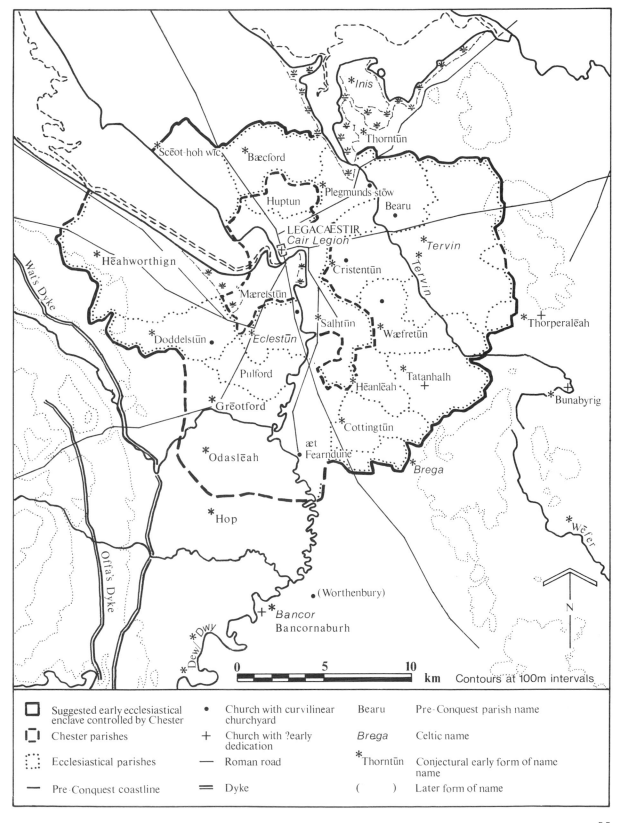

*Inis

Thorntūn

*Scēot·hoh wīc

*Bæcford

Plegmunds·stōw

Huptun

Bearu

LEGACAESTIR
Cair Legion

*Tervin

Tervin

*Hēahworthign

Cristentūn

Māerelstūn

Salhtūn

*Thorperalēah

*Eclestūn

*Wæfretūn

*Doddelstūn

Pulford

*Tatanhalh

*Hēanlēah

*Grēotford

*Bunabyrig

*Cottingtūn

æt
Fearndune

*Odaslēah

*Brega

*Hop

*Wēfer

(Worthenbury)

*Bancor
Bancornaburh

Wat's Dyke

Offa's Dyke

Dēw/Dwy

0   5   10
km   Contours at 100m intervals

N

	Suggested early ecclesiastical enclave controlled by Chester	•	Church with curvilinear churchyard	Bearu	Pre-Conquest parish name
	Chester parishes	+	Church with ?early dedication	*Brega*	Celtic name
	Ecclesiastical parishes	—	Roman road	*Thorntūn	Conjectural early form of name name
	Pre-Conquest coastline	=	Dyke	( )	Later form of name

33 *Sixth- or seventh-century 'pilgrim flask' found at Meols. It contained holy water from the shrine of St Menas in Egypt.*

may well have been the focus of Scandinavian settlement in the city.

Elsewhere, St John's Church remained an ecclesiastical centre. The area was known as the 'Bishop's borough' by the time of the Norman Conquest. There was also development along Foregate Street. The area west of the old Roman fortress does not seem to have been occupied, although a substantial settlement lay here in Roman times.

The Saxon buildings though widespread were usually thinly scattered, although the frontages of the major streets probably became fairly built up. To a certain extent the Saxon occupation seems to have fitted in and around surviving Roman ruins (**colour plate 4**). However, the nature of this occupation probably reflected choice as much as the impositions

of the site. By the time of the Norman Conquest, the Domesday Survey records a total of 508 houses in Chester.

The burh defences
Although archaeology has not yet revealed the line of the burghal defences, documentary and topographical clues suggest a probable course. This followed the northern and eastern walls of the Roman fortress, with two earthen spur ramparts joining the north-western and south-eastern corners of the fortress to the river, thus forming a defensive line in the shape of an inverted 'L'. Although they may no longer have been needed, the southern and western walls and gateways of the Roman fortress probably survived until the twelfth century.

The street plan
The deliberate foundation of new burhs brought with it a revival of town-planning based on a rectilinear grid. At Chester, the survival of much of the Roman fortress meant that the framework for the new town already existed. The principal streets of the fortress were retained and became the main thoroughfares of the Saxon, medieval and modern city (Eastgate Street, Watergate Street and Bridge Street). The northern third of Northgate Street was also Roman, but its southern part probably did not come into existence until the eleventh century. On the other hand, a great many lesser Roman streets were lost before or during the Saxon period, although some of them did remain in use, for example, the southern part of Crook Street.

Perimeter roads giving access to the defences were common features of Saxon burhs. A stretch of such a road was found at Abbey Green, and undated gravel tracks which have been found elsewhere along the northern and eastern sectors of the defences could have been part of the same system.

King Street, Princess Street and Newgate Street were important modifications to the Roman plan. All follow sinuous routes across the sites of Roman barrack blocks. King Street and Princess Street are probably post-Conquest in origin (see below, p. 65). Newgate Street, on the other hand, could well be Saxon.

Outside the fortress the main streets were again inherited from the Roman period: Lower Bridge Street running down to the bridge over the Dee (the Roman bridge probably remained in use), Foregate Street issuing out of the Eastgate and forming the principal route to the east and south, and Upper Northgate Street running northwards to the Wirral. As the western side of the city appears to have remained unoccupied in the Saxon period all the streets in this area are probably post-Conquest.

Some of the thoroughfares established in this period were not destined to survive. This includes some of sections of the perimeter road

34 *Plan of Chester in the tenth century, showing the conjectured line of burh defences, areas of densest settlement and the most substantial Roman ruins.*

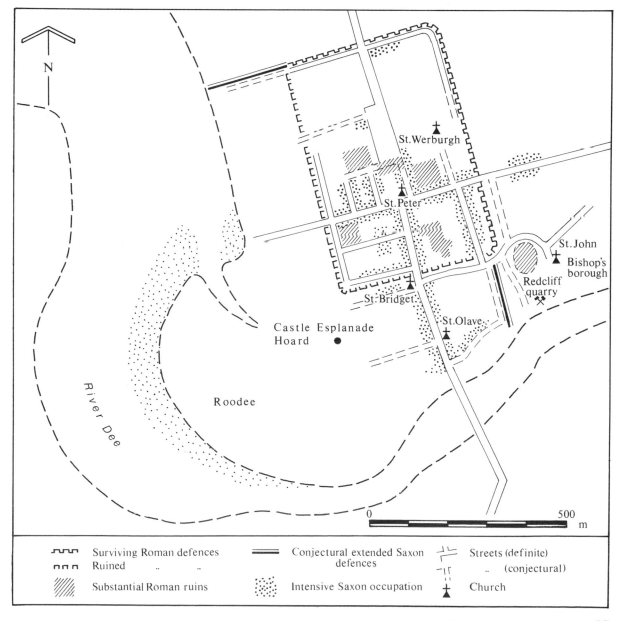

and a roughly-paved track about 36m (120ft) north of the present Princess Street. Perhaps if Princess Street had not come into existence at a later date, this track might have developed into a permanent thoroughfare.

Churches

Three churches, St John, St Werburgh and St Peter, are certainly pre-Conquest foundations. St John and St Werburgh were minsters with large parishes. As already noted, St John's was a seventh-century foundation, and St Werburgh's (in its guise as SS Peter and Paul) could also be very early. After the rededication to St Werburgh, part of the former dedication – to St Peter – was transferred to the church at the Cross. The dedications of St Bridget's and St Olave's suggest that they, too, were probably pre-Conquest foundations. The church of St Olave cannot pre-date the martyrdom of the Norwegian king of that name in 1030. No fabric from this period has been identified in any of the churches, but some of them at least were probably fine buildings in stone.

Domestic occupation

Parts of several buildings of this period have been found; most were primarily domestic. All were wooden and the evidence for them consists largely of post-holes and sometimes sunken areas. Fired daub survived from a workshop at Abbey Green which had burnt down. The superstructures of the other buildings were presumably perishable, probably timber and thatch.

Even in the small sample investigated, a wide range of accommodation types has been recovered, presumably representing a fair cross-section of society. Hall-type structures, found at Hunter's Walk and Crook Street, were the largest buildings. Cellared buildings have been found in Lower Bridge Street. Although smaller than the halls they were nevertheless still substantial buildings. The basements provided a secure storage or work room, while the upper floors could have provided living accommodation (**35**). Other buildings were partly sunken, with their main floors below ground level. Examples of these have been found in Lower Bridge Street and at Hamilton Place. Some were small and, with eaves resting on the ground, must have had limited headroom.

Industrial activity

At Abbey Green antler-working and possibly iron-smithing were carried on. The conduct of two such disparate activities close together on the northern periphery of the settlement may have been associated with the church of St Werburgh. This contrasts with the large-scale and more intensive eleventh-century tanning industry at Lower Bridge Street. There the cellared buildings were demolished and the site was given over to large pits and troughs for soaking skins. The former basements became filled with the residues of this activity. Below St John's was a quarry (hence the name 'Redcliff' for that part of the city) where masons produced crosses for the churchyard.

The Scandinavians in Chester

Place-name and documentary evidence suggests that the main concentration of Scandinavian settlement in Chester was in the southern part of the city. The cellared and semi-basement design of buildings on Lower Bridge Street were typical Scandinavian structural forms. However, an example of the type is also known from Hamilton Place.

Irish–Norse style metalwork – ring-headed pins and a brooch with an identical parallel from Dublin – have been found in the supposedly Saxon part of the settlement. Likewise the St John's crosses have parallels around the coasts of the Irish Sea. Conversely, Chester Ware pottery, which is certainly Saxon, is as commonly found in the supposedly Scandinavian area as it is elsewhere in the town.

In conclusion, therefore, although there is some documentary evidence to suggest that the southern part of the burh was inhabited by people of Scandinavian stock, and (by implication) the old fortress area by Saxons, it would

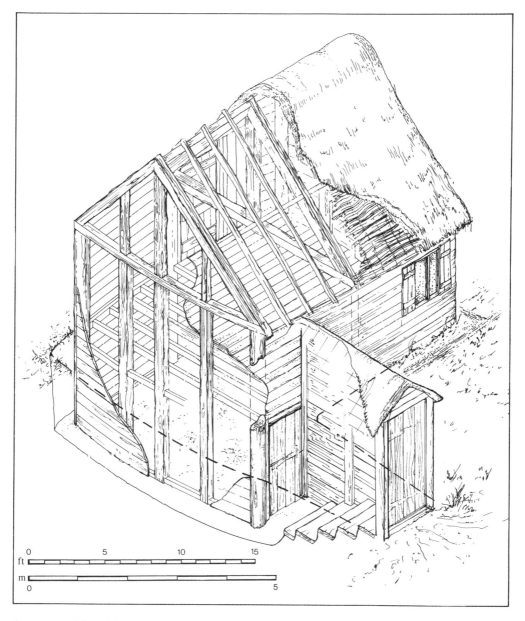

appear that a considerable degree of integration took place, with the fruits of trade equally available to both communities.

35 *Reconstruction drawing of a typical example of the Scandinavian-style cellared buildings found during excavations in Lower Bridge Street.*

The port

The evidence for the late Saxon port comes from documents, coins and some of the traded objects. Chester provided the English kings with a window on the Irish Sea trade, and the regulations governing the port which are recorded in the Domesday Survey and the spectacular rise of the Chester mint show their desire to control and profit from this trade.

Of all the routes converging on Chester, that from the Irish Sea into the English Midlands was the most important. Some of the finds from late Saxon Chester give a hint of its long-distance trading contacts. 'Chester Ware' pot-

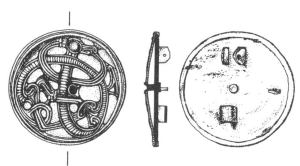

37 *Copper alloy disc brooch. The decoration consists of an interlacing ribbon-shaped animal, characteristic of the 'Jellinge' style of Viking art fashionable in the tenth century. Four examples of this particular design are known from areas of Viking activity in Britain, including Dublin, with which Chester had close links.*

36 *'Chester Ware' cooking pot found at Princess Street in 1981. Before it was introduced, about the beginning of the tenth century, scarcely any pottery had been used in Chester since Roman times. The ware is found widely through the West Midlands.*

38 *Carved bone strap-end found on the site of the Roman south-western angle tower. Tenth century. The decoration shows the 'Tree of Life' flanked by two birds. This motif, which was common both in Britain and on the Continent at that time, had its origins in the early civilizations of the Middle East.*

tery has been found in Viking Dublin, and the Chester mint-signature is the most common on English coins found in tenth-century Irish hoards.

The only imported items mentioned in the Domesday Survey are marten furs, but a book about Chester written by Lucian, a twelfth-century monk of St Werburgh's Abbey, refers to foodstuffs, including fish, from Ireland, cattle and sheep from Wales, and wine from Germany, Aquitaine and Spain. There was a trade in slaves between Chester and Dublin between the tenth and twelfth centuries, and the revival of the Cheshire salt industry at Nantwich in the tenth century may have brought further trade to the port.

The Saxon mint

From the end of the ninth century information about Chester increases considerably, thanks in part to the silver pennies produced by Chester's mint.

The manner in which coins were produced and circulated was one of the more curious developments in later Anglo-Saxon England. The kings of Wessex were attempting to draw the reins of power more closely in to their own hands, yet they chose to disperse the process of making coins from a handful of central mints to a large number of smaller ones in towns throughout their kingdom.

Chester was one such town (**40** and **41**). Its mint probably began production towards the end of the ninth century, before the foundation of the burh. Throughout most of the tenth century it was one of the most prolific in England. Normally, it ranked fifth after London in output, but there were several occasions when the number of moneyers working in the city rivalled the capital.

Peaks in production may indicate that large quantities of silver had suddenly become available to be minted – for example, it has been suggested that Aethelstan's capture of York in 928 provided a supply of silver in the form of booty which was then turned into coin at Chester.

The period when the mint's output was at its greatest coincided with the blossoming of trade between the lands bordering the Irish Sea. The large quantities of silver minted in the city helped to finance this booming trade with the Viking north, and Chester pennies

39 *Ring-headed copper alloy dress-pins from Chester and Meols. This style of pin was an Irish one much favoured by the Vikings.*

40 (Left) *Penny by the moneyer Thurmod (Thurmod. mo. in. Leg) from the reign of Edgar (959–75). (Right) Penny of Aethelred II (979–1016) by the Scandinavian moneyer Swegen.*

frequently found their way to Ireland and Scandinavia. It appears that the connection between Chester and Viking Dublin was particularly important – for example a pair of dies cut at Chester for a coin of the Dublin king Sihtric (921–7). The close ties between the city and Viking Ireland lasted until the end of the tenth century.

The mint's activities declined sharply in the 970s for reasons which are not clearly understood, and did not pick up again until the beginning of the next century. After 1000 Chester again began to produce coins in quantity, and its position as a major mint was maintained until the Norman Conquest and beyond. By this time, however, a significant part of the trade with Ireland had passed to Bristol, and the Chester mint was never able to regain the pre-eminence which it had enjoyed in the tenth century.

The practice of putting the moneyer's name on the reverse of each coin gives us an insight into the mixture of nationalities living in Chester during the later Saxon period. Not surprisingly, Saxon names make up the largest single group, but there are also significant numbers of others. Norse names make up something like a quarter of the total, for instance Raenulf in the reign of Aethelstan (925–39) and Thorald

41 (Left) *Penny of Aethelstan (924–39) by the moneyer Eadmund. The legend reads 'Aethelstan King of all Britain'.* (Right) *Penny by Maeldomen, from the same reign.*

under Aethelred II (979–1016). Other moneyers have Welsh or Irish names, such as Maeldomen, Maertin and Macsuthan; there are also a few Germans, possibly Franks, with names like Boiga and Durand.

Because of the sheer number of mints throughout the country it was necessary for each coin to bear some indication of where it was made as well as the name of the moneyer. Until as late as the beginning of the twelfth century the abbreviations used on the Chester coins indicate that the name of the city, officially at least, was LEGECAESTER – a direct translation of its Welsh name CARLEGION or CAERLEON meaning 'the fortress of the legion'. However, even before the Norman Conquest some manuscripts omitted the first part of the name, and by the time of Henry I the coinage had also simplified it to a form which is recognizable as 'Chester'.

The Chester coin series differed from the products of other Anglo-Saxon mints in various ways. Until the time of Edgar's reforms in 973, Chester coins did not carry the portrait of the king on the obverse; in its place a small central motif of a cross or a rosette was used. Another distinctive local feature was the celebration of the creation of the Aethelflaedan burh in 907 by a group of coins showing a stone tower. The new coins, although clearly based on a fourth-century Roman original, were obviously intended as a reference to the refurbishment of Chester's defences.

No building has been identified as the site of the Saxon mint, nor is there any indication as to where in the city it lay. This is not really surprising in view of the evidence which has come from the Coppergate area in York. There the traces of a die-manufacturing workshop, if not an actual mint, were found in the remains of two very ordinary-looking wooden buildings which by themselves would not have given a clue as to their function.

A Saxon jar containing a hoard of over 500 silver pennies, many of them from the Chester mint, was found in 1950 on the Castle Esplanade in the south-western part of the city (**42**). In addition to the coins there was a considerable

quantity of 'hacksilber' (small pieces of silver scrap), some of it recognizable as the remains of jewellery such as bracelets and brooches. There was also a number of silver ingots, some of which had been cut, along with some rather more carefully shaped discs which were clearly coin blanks. The total value of the coins, hacksilber and ingots adds up to something like 1300 pence – a very considerable sum of money in the tenth century; the hoard was probably hidden in the 970s. The find spot, between the Saxon burh and the river, has led to the suggestion that it was the property of a Viking trader who had left his ship and hidden his working capital before entering the Saxon settlement. Obviously something prevented him from retrieving it afterwards.

42 *'Hacksilber' and silver ingots from the Castle Esplanade coin hoard, concealed in the 970s, together with a stone ingot-mould found during excavations in Lower Bridge Street.*

5

Chester in the Medieval and Tudor Periods

Historical summary

In 1070, William the Conqueror, faced with a revolt in the northern parts of his newly-acquired realm, marched through Cheshire laying waste the countryside. When he arrived at Chester he built an earth and timber 'motte and bailey' style castle. He also established a strong earldom at Chester, together with others along the Welsh Marches based on Shrewsbury and Hereford.

The first earl was Hugh of Avranches, nick-named Lupus (the Wolf) or the Fat. He was followed by a further six earls. The last, John the Scot, died in 1237 without an heir, and the earldom was annexed by the Crown. Since 1254 the earldom has always been held by the monarch's eldest son. The earls held extensive lands throughout the country as well as most of Cheshire, and by astute political manoeuvring they became powerful figures. The fourth earl, Ranulf II of Gernons (1129–53), and the sixth, Ranulf III (1181–1232), were the most notable.

In spite of the wealth and influence of the earls, Chester itself remained relatively small. The basis of wealth at this time was land and agriculture, and as Cheshire has mostly heavy clay soils which were difficult to farm it did not support a large population. Nor did the annexation of the earldom by the Crown bring any particular benefit to the city. The royal earls tended to consider the earldom merely as a source of revenue or an opportunity for patronage, and rarely visited the city.

Through the first two centuries after the Norman Conquest Chester grew slowly. Its population at the time of the Domesday Survey in 1086 was no more than perhaps 1500. In the later thirteenth century, Henry III and his son Edward I mounted campaigns in Wales. Edward consolidated the conquest by constructing the chain of castles including Conwy, Caernarfon and Beaumaris, which are still impressive features of the Welsh coastline. All the armies, workmen and supplies to mount the campaigns and build the castles passed through Chester. It is not surprising, therefore, that this was the most prosperous period for the city during the Middle Ages.

This prosperity was followed in 1349 by the Black Death, which affected Chester as severely as the rest of the country. The population fell by as much as a third and the economy stagnated. Few new buildings were erected. During this time the silting of the river at Chester became a serious problem, and it became increasingly difficult for ships to reach the quays at the city. When Richard II was deposed by Henry Bolingbroke (who thereby became Henry IV) in 1399 he was seized by the new king at Flint Castle and brought in chains to Chester before being incarcerated at Pontefract Castle.

During the fifteenth century the wars in France and the Wars of the Roses between the Lancastrian and Yorkist claimants to the throne largely passed Chester by, although they no doubt had an adverse effect on trade.

The city

The plan of the city was principally the one that had been inherited from the Saxons and from the Romans before them (**43**). The main streets remained the same; the existing defences were incorporated into the new work and three of the main gates and the Dee Bridge lay on the same sites. Even the major churches were Saxon foundations. However, many new, typically medieval, institutions were founded in this period. These included the Castle, the monastic houses and the Rows. The streets giving access to the hitherto-undeveloped western side of the city, Nicholas Street and St Martin's Field, may also have been laid out in this period, as were King Street and Princess Street. The former, previously known as 'Barn Lane', gave access from Northgate Street to the tithe barn of St Werburgh's Abbey somewhere in the north-western corner of the city. The latter, formerly 'Parson's Lane', gave access from the Abbey Gateway to the house of the rector of St Oswald's (who until the 1340s used the nave of the abbey for his church).

In general, in the city centre buildings lay end-on to the street frontages and were packed tightly together, although there was much open ground behind them. By contrast, the western part of the city failed to develop commercially. It became known as the Crofts, being used for orchards, allotments and market gardening, and much of it was given away piecemeal to the religious orders.

The institutions of the city

At this time, the system of local government grew up which has continued to evolve to the present day. The Sheriffs, of whom there were two, date from at least 1121–9. By 1229 there was a Mayor chosen from the leading citizens, who formed the Corporation. The Mayor and Corporation had rights to regulate trade, collect tolls and try minor offences. These rights of self-government were confirmed by a charter of Edward the Black Prince in 1354 and the Great Charter of Henry VII in 1506.

The first Town Hall was the Moot Hall or Common Hall, which lay in Commonhall Street. By 1510, the City Assembly had moved to the old St Nicholas Chapel in Northgate Street, and the Common Hall became the chapel for St Ursula's Hospital. Courts and meetings were also held at the Pentice, a substantial two-storey structure built against St Peter's Church at the Cross.

The right to trade in the city was dependent on membership of the guild merchant and of the craft guilds which grew up somewhat later. Each trade – bakers, brewers, butchers, tanners, shoemakers, water carriers and so on – had a guild. The guilds also put on the famous cycle of Chester Mystery Plays at Whitsun. Each guild was responsible for a particular Bible story. They vied with each other to produce the most spectacular stage sets on the carts which travelled round the city performing the plays.

Two fairs were held in Chester, one in midsummer, controlled by the abbot, and the other at Michaelmas in the autumn. In addition there were regular markets in Eastgate Street by St Peter's Church.

The Castle

The Castle was built by William the Conqueror in 1070 in the south-western corner of the city, where it could command the bridge and port area. It conformed to the normal motte and bailey design. The motte was an earth mound which was surmounted by a timber tower. The bailey was an attached enclosure, defended by a ditch, bank and palisade, and contained the main living accommodation. The outline of the motte can still be seen, although its profile has been modified by later work. The original bailey probably corresponded with what is now the inner bailey (**44**).

The Castle became the headquarters of the earldom. Unfortunately, few records survive

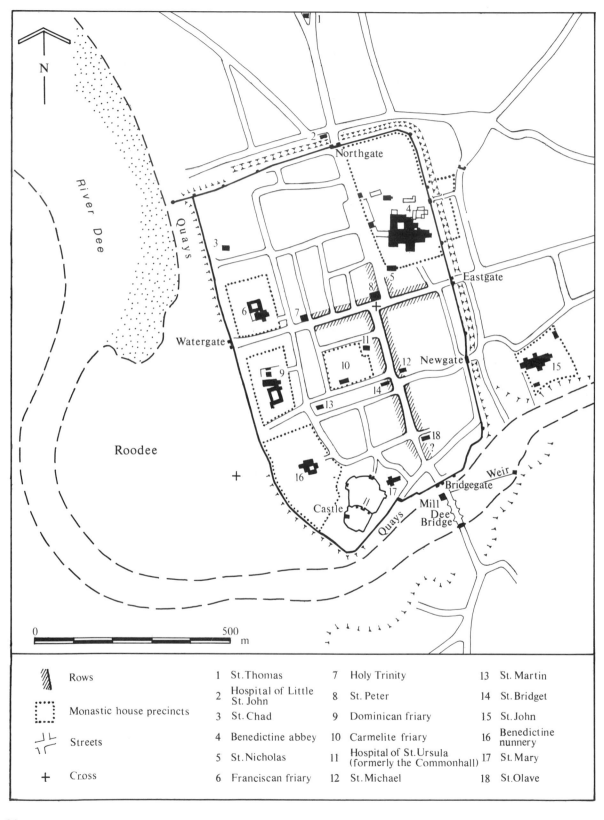

▨	Rows	1	St. Thomas	7	Holy Trinity	13	St. Martin

Key:

- ▨ Rows
- ⬚ Monastic house precincts
- ⊥ Streets
- + Cross

1 St. Thomas
2 Hospital of Little St. John
3 St. Chad
4 Benedictine abbey
5 St. Nicholas
6 Franciscan friary
7 Holy Trinity
8 St. Peter
9 Dominican friary
10 Carmelite friary
11 Hospital of St. Ursula (formerly the Commonhall)
12 St. Michael
13 St. Martin
14 St. Bridget
15 St. John
16 Benedictine nunnery
17 St. Mary
18 St. Olave

43 *Plan of Chester in the Middle Ages.*

from the period before the earldom was taken over by the Crown, so we have only vague indications of the way in which the Castle developed. During the twelfth century the tower on the motte was rebuilt in stone. The bailey wall was also rebuilt in stone and provided with an impressive gate tower, now known as the Agricola Tower (**45** and **colour plate 5**). During this period the outer bailey was presumably added, although it was only surrounded by a bank and palisade.

Perhaps in the early thirteenth century a new gateway with two drum towers was built for the inner ward. The gate through the Agricola Tower was walled up. Henry III built a stone wall around the outer bailey in 1247–51, a new chamber in 1246–7 and the Great Hall in 1250–3. Edward I added chambers for the king and queen from 1283 and a new outer gatehouse in 1292–3. This completed the major work on the Castle in the Middle Ages,

44 *Plan of Chester Castle as it existed in the late Middle Ages.*

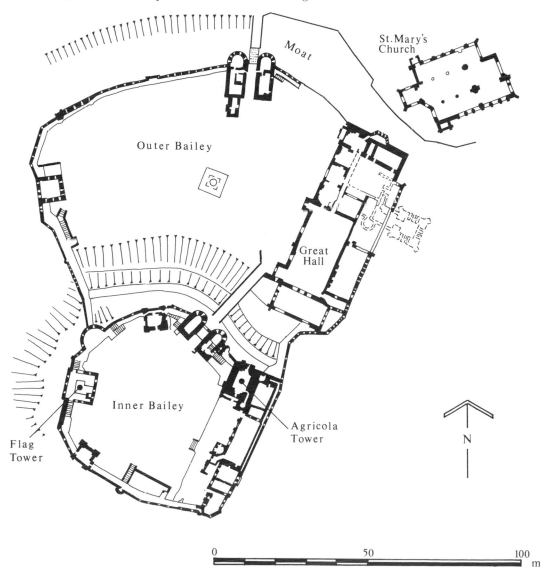

but the records show that it continued to be maintained. Although rarely used by the earl, it remained the centre of the administration of the earldom and housed his various officials and courts.

The outer bailey of the Catle was completely rebuilt during the late eighteenth century. Much medieval work remains in the inner bailey, including the Agricola Tower and the tower on the motte, now known as the Flag Tower.

The City Walls

The extension of the Roman circuit was completed by the Norman earls. During the 1120s they built the southern stretch of the Walls, including the Bridgegate and Shipgate. The western side was built in the second half of the twelfth century. No doubt the existing walls along the northern and eastern sides were also repaired. This produced the circuit of about 3km (2 miles) which survives today.

The curtain wall was only one element in an integrated defensive system which also included towers, gates, ditch and outworks. The towers and ditch occur only on the northern and eastern sides, which are not protected by the river. There were about ten towers altogether, built in a variety of designs. Some were rectangular, some rounded; some were solid and some contained chambers. Most survive, although some are very ruinous. Unlike the Roman ones, they projected forward from the walls to provide flanking fire.

The most interesting and impressive tower is the Water Tower at the north-western corner of the city, which was built in 1323. It is attached to the main circuit by a spur wall. When built, it stood in the river and protected the quays which lay under the Walls at this point. As the river silted up it became stranded on the shore and today it lies about 200m (650ft) from the bank.

None of the medieval gates survive; all were replaced during the eighteenth century to provide better access for traffic. We know a

45 *The 'Agricola Tower', originally the gate tower to the inner bailey of Chester Castle. The chapel, which has revealed some fine wall-paintings, is on the first floor. Despite its name, the tower has no Roman connections.*

good deal about their appearance, however, from seventeenth- and eighteenth-century illustrations. The Eastgate and Northgate lay on the sites of their Roman predecessors. The Eastgate, as befitted the main entrance to the city, was an impressive tall tower with low flanking towers (**46**). Four turrets projected from its front face. Its similarities to the King's Gate at Caernarfon Castle perhaps indicate that it was built in the early fourteenth century. The Northgate was a rectangular tower with a narrow gate passage through it (**47**). In the later Middle Ages it served as the city gaol.

The Bridgegate had two drum towers flanking the entrance passage (**48**). The Watergate was a simple arched opening in the Walls (**49**). The proximity of the river bank and quays here

46 *Reconstruction drawing of the medieval Eastgate, based on old illustrations and the results of excavations in 1972.*

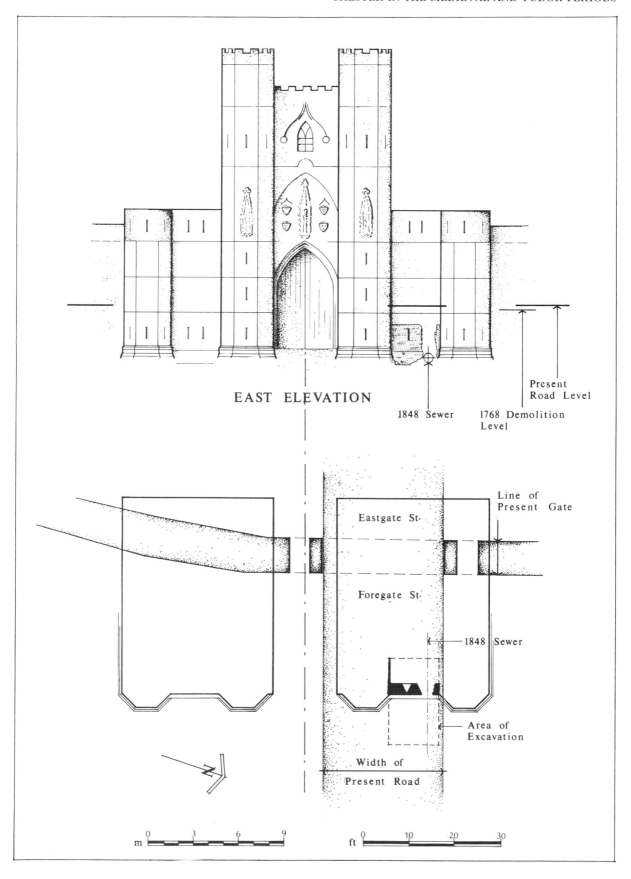

EAST ELEVATION

1848 Sewer

1768 Demolition
Level

Present
Road Level

Line of
Present Gate

Eastgate St.

Foregate St.

1848 Sewer

Area of
Excavation

Width of
Present Road

N

m 0   3   6   9

ft 0   10   20   30

presumably made a tower unnecessary. The two lesser gates, the Shipgate and the Newgate, were also simple arched openings. The Shipgate has been re-erected in the Grosvenor Park.

There were a few minor side gates. The best known is the Kaleyard Gate, near the abbey. This was built by the monks in 1275 to gain easier access to their vegetable garden, which lay just outside the City Walls.

Outside the Walls on the landward sides a ditch was dug. Recent excavations just to the north of the Eastgate have shown that three ditches in all were dug during the medieval period. They lay further out from the Walls

47 *The medieval Northgate, from an eighteenth- or early nineteenth-century pen and ink drawing.*

48 *The medieval Bridgegate, an etching by J. Stuart made shortly before its demolition. The water tower was added in 1607 by John Tyrer.*

than the Roman ditch in order to allow space for the projecting towers. The earliest ditch dates from about 1200 and measured 7m (23ft) wide and 1.25m (4ft) deep. It rapidly filled up with rubbish, and so it became necessary to dig another ditch. This was narrower but deeper than the first, measuring $3.5 \times 2m$ ($11\frac{1}{2} \times 6\frac{1}{2}$ft). It, too, became choked with rubbish. The final ditch was much smaller, measuring only about 0.9m (3ft) deep.

49 (Right, below) *Lithograph of the medieval Watergate.*

Outworks

Outside the main circuit of the Walls there were three outworks. The Bars lay at the end of Foregate Street and marked the city limits in that direction. The Cow Lane Gate lay at the northern end of Cow Lane, now Frodsham Street. Both of these gates were merely walls across the streets butted up to the adjoining houses and pierced by an archway. Their sites survive as place-names.

The outer Bridgegate at the southern end of the Old Dee Bridge was a serious defence work, however, as befitted one bestriding the main route into North Wales. The site of this gateway is still marked by the southernmost pier of the bridge, which is considerably larger than the rest. The gate itself was demolished in 1782.

Churches

Like most medieval cities, Chester had numerous churches. There were eight parish churches, the large Benedictine abbey of St Werburgh's (which also served as the head of the parish of St Oswald), a Benedictine nunnery and three friaries. There were also three hospitals which operated on similar lines to religious institutions.

Two of the parish churches (St John's and St Peter's) are known to have been founded before the Norman Conquest, as probably do two more (St Olave's and St Bridget's). The remainder (Holy Trinity, St Michael's, St Martin's and St Mary's) are post-Conquest.

St John's was the earliest parish church and was the most important throughout the Middle Ages. In 1075 Bishop Peter moved his seat from Lichfield to Chester and raised St John's to cathedral status. He started building a fine large church, but it was still incomplete when he died in 1085 (**50**). The seat of the diocese then moved again, first to Coventry and finally back to Lichfield. The upper storeys of the nave of the church were built in the late twelfth century. One bay of the choir, the crossing and the nave of this magnificent Romanesque and early Gothic church survive (**colour plate 8**). The eastern chapels, rebuilt in the thirteenth

50 *Lead seal of Peter, Bishop of Chester 1075–85. Bishops' seals were normally of silver and were broken on their death. This may be a contemporary copy.*

and fourteenth centuries, now stand as ruins outside the church. The great western tower, for long a dominant feature of Chester's skyline, collapsed in 1881 – only its stump remains.

St Peter's occupies a prominent central position in Chester at the Cross. During the Middle Ages the church was closely associated with the civic authorities. The Pentice, which served as the Town Hall, was built against its southern and eastern sides. The present building dates to the fourteenth and fifteenth centuries.

St Mary's was founded as the church for the Castle. The original chapel in the Castle (St Mary de Castro) lay on the first floor of the Agricola Tower. However, because of the growing number of parishioners, a new church, St Mary on the Hill, was built immediately outside the Castle. It is a late medieval building with a fine timber roof over the nave and several tombs of important Chester families.

Of the surviving parish churches, only St Peter's and St John's continue in ecclesiastical use. Holy Trinity and St Michael's were rebuilt during the last century and are currently used as the Guild-hall and the City Council's Heritage Centre respectively. St Olave's is an interesting small aisle-less medieval building. St Bridget's and St Martin's no longer exist, both having been lost to new road schemes.

St Werburgh's Abbey

In 1092 Earl Hugh Lupus refounded the Saxon minster of St Werburgh as a Benedictine abbey. This act can be seen as part of the effort to reform the church in England on the most up-to-date lines. It was also a major element in the imposition of Norman rule on the capital of the new earldom. Monks from the prestigious monastery at Bec in Normandy were brought over to form the core of the new establishment. The abbey was richly endowed with income and land, including all the north-eastern quarter of the city, which became the abbey precinct.

Building work commenced immediately and had progressed far enough for Earl Hugh to be buried there when he died in 1101. The Romanesque north transept, the north-western tower and the intervening cloister wall with its finely decorated doorway still survive from this first church.

However, most of the fabric of the church that can be seen today is the product of a long building campaign which began in the mid-thirteenth century with the Lady Chapel at the eastern end (**51**). This programme was carried on intermittently until the western end was reached in the sixteenth century. Work was only halted by the Dissolution in 1540. Consequently, there is a rich variety of styles represented in the building (**52**). As the Cheshire

51 *Plan of St Werburgh's Abbey. 'St Oswald's' was originally the chapel of St Nicholas, but was used by the parishioners of St Oswald's from the mid-fourteenth century.*

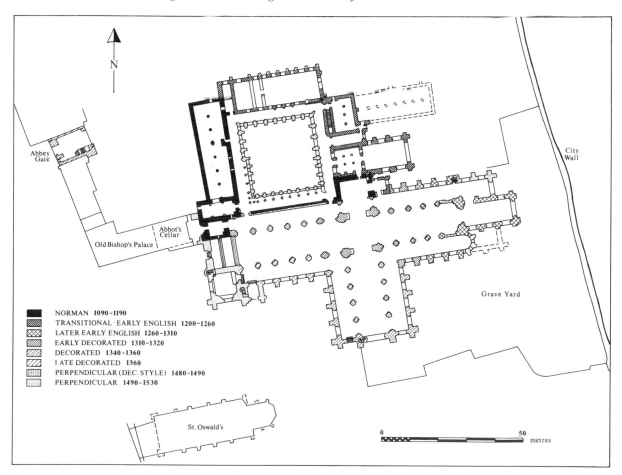

NORMAN 1090-1190
TRANSITIONAL–EARLY ENGLISH 1200-1260
LATER EARLY ENGLISH 1260-1310
EARLY DECORATED 1310-1320
DECORATED 1340-1360
LATE DECORATED 1360
PERPENDICULAR (DEC. STYLE) 1480-1490
PERPENDICULAR 1490-1530

Abbey Gate

Abbot's Cellar

Old Bishop's Palace

City Wall

Grave Yard

St. Oswald's

0   50 metres

sandstone is soft and weathers easily, the exterior has been heavily restored. The interior stonework, however, is original.

The mid-thirteenth-century Lady Chapel is in Early English style. It contains a shrine to St Werburgh which was demolished during the Reformation but reconstructed in the nineteenth century from the surviving pieces. The choir is in the Decorated Gothic style. The work of at least four master masons has been identified in the choir and crossing, including that of Richard the Engineer, who worked on Caernarfon Castle. By 1340 work had moved on to the south transept. This is very large – equal in size to the choir – to compensate for the north transept, which was constricted by the presence of the cloister.

There was a break in building work in the later fourteenth century. When work was resumed on the nave it was built in the Perpendicular style. The ornate west front was completed about 1500. The upper parts of the south-western tower and porch, however, were never finished.

One of the finest and most important features in the church are the magnificent wooden choir stalls. They were carved in about 1390 by very skilled craftsmen, perhaps in royal employment.

The abbey also boasts one of the most complete groups of monastic buildings in the country, arranged around a cloister. The Chapter House and its vestibule are both fine early thirteenth-century work. The monks' dorter, or dormitory, on the first floor of the eastern range has not survived. However, the lower part of the day stairs which once led up to it can still be seen.

The frater, or refectory, lies in the northern range. This magnificent hall still contains the pulpit, built into the wall, from which the monks listened to a daily reading while they ate in silence. In the cloister walk by the door to the frater is a stone shelf which once housed the lavabo, or sink, in which the monks washed their hands.

The western range, like the eastern, has lost

its upper storey. The lower floor is a fine Norman vaulted cellar used as the storeroom for the abbey. The upper floor once contained the abbot's lodging. Now only his chapel, dedicated to St Anselm, survives. This was refitted in the early seventeenth century. As the abbots grew in wealth and power, their lodging was extended into a range extending out westwards from the church and forming the southern side of the abbey court. The site is currently occupied by a bank.

West of the cloister lay the outer court of the abbey, where workshops, bakehouses and brewhouses, stables and barns would have been situated. The court was turned into the elegant Abbey Square in Georgian times, but is still entered by the medieval Abbey Gateway, again thought to be the work of Richard the Engineer.

52 *The Romanesque north transept, one of the few parts of the eleventh-century abbey to survive.*

Relations between the city and the abbey were often not good. A continuing cause of difficulty was the fact that the abbey also served as the parish church of St Oswald. From the mid-fourteenth century the parishioners used a chapel dedicated to St Nicholas in the south-western corner of the precinct. This was extended in 1488. Subsequently, the parishioners moved back into the abbey church, using the large south transept. However, the chapel survives, having served later as the Common Hall, the wool hall, a theatre, a music hall, a cinema, a supermarket and a clothes shop!

The most famous member of the abbey was Ranulf Higden (entered 1299, died 1363–4). He wrote numerous religious works, but is chiefly remembered for the *Polychronicon*, a history of the world and England from the Creation to his own day in seven volumes. This became the standard work of history during the later Middle Ages.

The nunnery

The Benedictine nunnery was founded by Earl Ranulph II about 1150 on land in the western part of the city, immediately north of the Castle. It was never a large or wealthy house. We know a certain amount about it from a seventeenth-century plan and from excavations. The County Police Headquarters now occupies its site.

It had a normal monastic plan, with a church with one aisle to the north of the cloister. After the Dissolution a house was built in the outer court. At the time of the Civil War this belonged to Sir William Brereton, the commander of the Parliamentary forces in Cheshire, and was pillaged by the city's Royalist garrison. Thereafter the site remained derelict, the last ruins of the church only being cleared away in 1800. However, the chancel arch has survived and has been re-erected in the Grosvenor Park.

The friaries

During the Middle Ages there were three friaries in Chester. Introduced into this country during the thirteenth century, the friars represented a break with established monastic tradition. Instead of forming a closed community, cut off from the world and dedicated to a life of worship, the friars went out into the world, preaching and ministering to the poor and needy. In consequence, they achieved a great popularity at a time when the established monasteries were being increasingly seen as lax, rich and worldly.

The Chester House of the Dominicans or Black Friars was founded about 1236. They were granted a large block of land on the western side of the city, north of the nunnery, between Black Friars Lane and Watergate Street (**colour plate 9**).

Excavations have revealed the northern half of the church and the buildings in the court to the north of it. The cloister, whose existence is known from documents, is thought to have lain to the south. The church was rebuilt on four occasions and developed from a simple aisle-less structure to a large and complex structure. Many of those buried in it were clearly members of the public, as they included women and children.

North of the church was a fine timber-framed building, which might have been the prior's lodging or the guest quarters. East of this were two large subterranean masonry structures, which may have been reservoirs; in 1276, the friars petitioned the king to allow them to lay a water conduit to the friary from Boughton, about 3km (2 miles) east of Chester.

After the Dissolution, a house was built on the site of the cloister and the friary buildings were demolished piecemeal over a period of about a century. The house survives in a much-altered form as the confusingly named Greyfriars House. This name, together with that of the access lane called Grey Friars, came about as a result of antiquarian speculation about the sites of the two friaries.

The Franciscans or Grey Friars arrived in Chester in 1237, close on the heels of the Dominicans, and were settled on another block of land on the western side of the city, north of Watergate Street. No remains of the Grey Friars' house survive above ground. Discoveries made during building work revealed a section across the frater, cloister garth and church. Various documents, including a seventeenth-century plan, give further information. These suggest a large church with aisled nave, a prominent south transept and a narrow choir. The cloister lay to the north, with an outer court to the west of it. There was possibly a large lesser cloister north of the main one, containing among other buildings the Infirmary.

The Grey Friars suffered from severe financial difficulties during the early sixteenth century and were obliged to lease out much of their property. In 1528, they allowed the Merchants and Sailors of Chester to store their sails and equipment in the nave which they had recently built in return for maintaining the church. Presumably the friars found the choir was sufficient for their needs.

The Carmelites or White Friars arrived last. A community existed by 1277 when Edward I gave them alms. However, it was not until 1290 that Hugh Payne, a local citizen, gave them the land in White Friars on which they built their church. At the Dissolution they were the most prosperous of the three friaries.

The church lay alongside White Friars lane on the southern side of the precinct, so the cloister presumably lay to the north of it. In 1495 an elegant tower and steeple were built, which were pulled down with the other remains of the church in 1592. A tiled floor and part of an apse found near the eastern end of White Friars may have been part of the church. White Friars, an eighteenth- and nineteenth-century house at the western end of the precinct, incorporates medieval sandstone walling.

With the establishment of the White Friars the complement of churches in medieval Chester was complete. They were a very significant feature of the city. Their precincts accounted for almost a quarter of the land within the City Walls. To this may be added the large block of land held by St John's. However, their significance was not confined to the area they occupied; the large, stone-built structures must have dominated the skyline of the city: St Werburgh's Abbey, which survives as the cathedral, is still one of the largest buildings in Chester.

Hospitals

During the Middle Ages hospitals provided accommodation and support for the elderly, sick or infirm. They were generally established as charities and were governed by rules similar to the religious orders. There were three hospitals in Chester.

St Giles in Boughton was a leper hospital. It lay about 1.5km (1 mile) to the east of the city centre, its isolated position reflecting the fear that the disease aroused in people in medieval times. It may have been in existence by 1181. It was granted considerable privileges, including the right to collect tolls on all food brought for sale in Chester. By the end of the Middle Ages it appears that the inhabitants were not sick, but able-bodied, and that people could inherit places in it. The hospital was demolished during the Civil War in 1643. The site of its graveyard may still be seen today on the southern side of Christleton Road.

St John the Baptist, also known as Little St John's to distinguish it from the church of St John's, lay immediately outside the North-gate. It was founded in the 1190s by Earl Ranulph III. Throughout the Middle Ages it provided accommodation for thirteen inmates. It often experienced financial difficulty through bad administration; like St Giles, it, too, was demolished during 1644. However, the hospital was re-established after the Civil War under the auspices of the city. The Blue Coat Charity School and chapel erected in 1717 stand on its site.

St Ursula's Hospital lay in Commonhall Street. It was found in 1510, following a bequest by Roger Smith. Six almshouses were built and the disused Common Hall behind them was converted into a chapel. As a religious institution the hospital was dissolved by Act of

Parliament in 1547. The almshouses continued in use, however, and the buildings were finally demolished in 1871.

The Dissolution

The Dissolution of the religious houses by Henry VIII was a major event in the development of the city and marks a clear break with the Middle Ages. For some time before the Dissolution the friaries in particular had been suffering from poverty and had leased out much of their land. A decline in the number of people choosing the religious life, and falling alms and bequests all meant that they were no longer the force that they had once been. In Chester, therefore, the Dissolution did not create any great local opposition. The three friaries were all surrendered to the king's commissioners on the same day in 1538. The abbey and nunnery survived until 1540. In the following year the abbey was refounded as the cathedral for the new diocese of Chester and the Dean and Chapter were granted the lands in Chester that had been held by the abbey.

The lands of the other religious houses were acquired by wealthy Chester citizens or local gentry, who built themselves large town houses in extensive grounds, very different from the medieval houses crammed tightly along the street frontages in the heart of the city. Even today, the former precincts support a more spacious and grander style of townscape.

The Rows

The Rows are Chester's most famous architectural feature. They are found on the four main streets – Bridge Street (formerly Lower Bridge Street as well), Watergate Street, Eastgate Street and the part of Northgate Street closest to the Cross. They consist of continuous galleries which run through the fronts of the buildings at first-floor level. On one side they are open to the street; on the other they provide a second level of commercial frontage to the properties. Access to them is gained by flights of steps set at irregular intervals (**53** and **colour plate 10**).

The Row buildings were constructed on undercrofts which have their floors at street level. The undercrofts have sandstone walls, the best examples having stone vaults or arcades to support a thick earth and flagged floor above; others have massive timber ceilings. They were used mainly as shops and warehouses.

On the same floor as the Row walkway was the hall. This was the main living room and was open to the roof. The largest halls were built parallel to the street across several undercrofts. Smaller examples lay at right-angles, directly over one undercroft. The halls were at first heated by a central hearth, hence the need for thick, heavy floors. Later, fireplaces with chimneys were built at one side of the hall. At the front of the hall there were one or more shops opening from the Row. Above the Row lay the main private chamber, the solar. Further chambers might lie at the back of the hall above the service rooms and the kitchen. These residential rooms and shops were often in different ownership from the undercroft beneath.

Behind the buildings lay yards and gardens. The ground level of these yards was at the level of the Row rather than the street. This distinctive feature is largely the product of Roman and later building- and occupation-debris raising the ground in these areas, while the streets remained at the same level.

Recent studies have shown that the Rows have existed more or less in the form they are today from at least the mid-thirteenth century. These studies have also discovered that a much larger number of medieval structures survives than was previously believed. Over the centuries new frontages were added, but behind them the old cores of buildings were usually altered and adapted rather than completely rebuilt, and their medieval appearance can often be conjectured from what remains.

The basic arrangement of the Row buildings is not unusual in medieval architecture. However, whereas elsewhere the undercrofts would

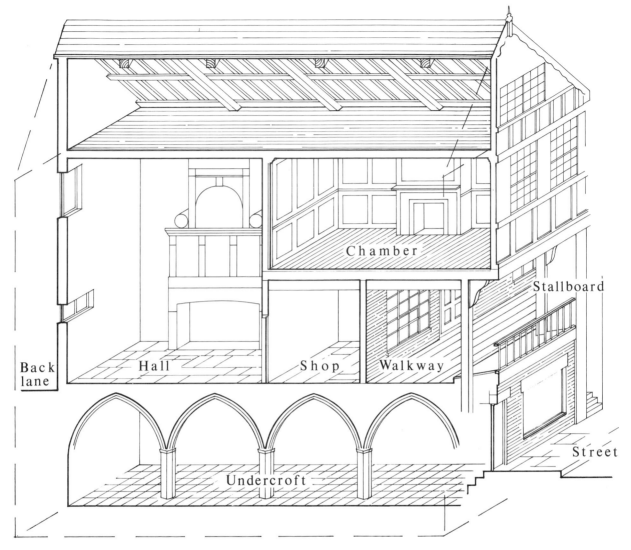

53 *Cut-away view of a typical Row building.*

have been completely underground, at Chester they were built at street level. This was probably done partly because the natural rock was very close to the surface and partly because the build-up of debris raised the ground level away from the streets. As the street frontages gradually built up, it became practical to link the galleries above the undercrofts to form a continuous Row. A disastrous fire in 1278 and the prosperity generated by Edward I's Welsh campaigns may have given an impetus to their development.

Other domestic buildings

Buildings similar to the Row buildings but without the walkway lay along the other streets and lanes of Chester. Arcaded buildings, where the first floor projects forward over the pavement, were particularly common in Foregate Street. There must also have been smaller cottages for the poorer classes, but these do not survive.

The port

Chester's situation was in many ways ideal for its development as a major port during the Middle Ages. This potential was never realized, however, for two main reasons. Firstly, the river Dee is a very actively silting river and there were continual difficulties in keeping it navigable. Secondly, there was neither a large population nor a rich agricultural base in the immediate hinterland of the city which was able to support extensive trading links. In particular, wool, which was England's main export, was not traded through Chester.

Nevertheless, the port was an important element of the local economy. On the west coast it was second only to Bristol and operated as Head Port for all the harbours in North Wales and north-western England. Chester merchants were active in the wine trade with Gascony in south-western France, and, following a treaty in 1466, trade developed with Spain.

Iron, oil, wine, cork and food stuffs were imported, while cheap cloth and hides were exported. A second strand to trade was that with Ireland, particularly Dublin. This included the instruments of government – officials, troops and money. Goods such as salt, salted fish, corn and metals were also traded. Finally, local coastal trade was always important. From the late thirteenth century, this included the supply of the castles on the North Wales coast.

54 *Map of Chester by John Speed, c. 1610, inset in a map of the county. This is the earliest reliable map of the city. Note the open ground behind the street frontages, and also that most of the remains of the religious houses have already disappeared.*

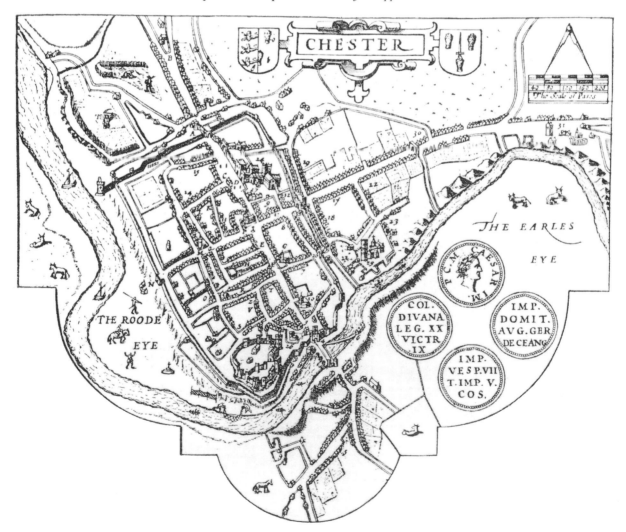

The quays at Chester were situated in two areas. Those on the southern side, by the Old Dee Bridge, were reached by the Shipgate. On the western side they lay along the City Walls north of the Watergate. Silting throughout the Middle Ages and the increasing size of ships made these quays harder to use. Nowadays, the whole area of the former head of the estuary is dry land, known as the Roodee, and the present head lies some 12km (7½ miles) downstream. In the later Middle Ages increasing use was made of outports along the Wirral shore, such as Shotwick, Redbank, Burton, Parkgate and Heswall. Despite these expedients, by the end of the Middle Ages Liverpool was becoming a significant competitor and completely overshadowed Chester thereafter.

Castles

In the decades following the Norman Conquest a number of castles were built to guard the frontier with Wales. They were of the normal motte-and-bailey type, like Chester Castle, and were constructed of earth and timber. Shotwick castle lay north of Chester, guarding the lowest fording point of the Dee. Doddleston, Pulford and Aldford lay to the south of the city, with Castleton, Malpas and Oldcastle in the south of the county. Most were built by minor lords and were abandoned relatively quickly. Shotwick, however, was held by the earl and subsequently the king. It remained important, serving as a base for military expeditions into Wales and to Ireland, and was rebuilt in stone. Its importance declined following the peace with Wales in 1281 but it still survives as a set of prominent earthworks.

Beeston Castle, 15km (9 miles) south-east of Chester, was built on an isolated crag dominating the gap in the Mid-Cheshire Ridge through which passed the main route from Chester to the south-east. It was built in 1220 by Earl Ranulph III on his return from the Crusades and is still an impressive site.

The countryside

The area around Chester was dotted with manors and small villages in the Middle Ages and the majority of the villages survive. A series of aerial photographs taken by the Royal Air Force in 1947 revealed a remarkable medieval landscape with large areas of ridge and furrow overlain by more recent enclosed fields. Cheshire is generally considered to have been a largely pastoral county, and the ridge and furrow may have been created to facilitate drainage rather than being evidence for arable farming. Unfortunately, the majority of the ridge and furrow earthworks which existed in 1947 have now disappeared, the victim of modern farming practices.

The poverty of the countryside is shown by the number of townships in each ecclesiastical parish. In the south of England most communities were wealthy enough to endow their own parish church. However, in Cheshire few communities were able to do so, and it is common to find three or more townships sharing a church, which might consequently be some distance from the settlements.

A final typical medieval feature of the area is moated sites. These consist of rectangular platforms surrounded by a substantial moat, still frequently wet. Originally the platforms would have had a manor house built on them, but they are now mostly bare, the farm having moved to a more convenient site nearby. They generally date from the late Middle Ages. Huntington Old Hall Farm, about 4km (2½ miles) south-east of Chester, is a particularly good example. During the Middle Ages it was owned by St Werburgh's Abbey.

The Chester leather trade and industry

Leather played an important part in the medieval and post-medieval economy of Chester. This was not particularly unusual in pre-industrial Britain, where leather was used for a variety of goods, such as shoes, clothes, horse equipment, bottles, bags, belts and straps, which today might be made of synthetic

1 Roman Chester as it might have appeared from the south-west. The painting pre-dates discoveries in the centre of the fortress made between 1979 and 1981 and so differs slightly from the plan (**11**) (D. Swarbrick)

2 Reconstruction painting of the northern defences of the Roman fortress in the late first century. In the early second century a stone facing was added to the front and the towers and gateways were rebuilt in stone (T. Morgan).

3 Reconstruction painting of the interior of a centurion's quarters of the First Cohort, as it appeared in the late first and early second centuries. The decoration is based on fragments of painted wall plaster found in Roman demolition debris during excavations in Crook Street. The pattern is a simplified version of one that was common at that time in Italy and the north-western provinces (G. Sumner).

4 Chester as it might have appeared from the south-west in the late tenth century. In reality there would have been more houses – 508 are recorded in the Domesday Survey (D. Astley and A. M. Beckett).

5 Painting of Chester Castle by Moses Griffiths, as it existed in the last quarter of the eighteenth century. On the far left is the Great Hall in the Outer Bailey; in the centre is the early thirteenth-century gateway to the Inner Bailey, and to its left the rectangular Agricola Tower.

6 The Visitation, painted on the chapel vault of the Agricola Tower in Chester Castle. This scene belongs to a fragmentary but very important programme of paintings which probably date from the time of Earl Ranulf III (died 1232), or from soon after the earldom and Castle were taken over by King Henry III in 1237.

7 Two exquisite heads on the west wall of the chapel, including that of the Bishop of Adana (southern Turkey). They come from a largely destroyed scene showing the legend of Theophilus – the priest who sold his soul to the devil, but had it retrieved by the Virgin Mary. Other fragmentary scenes on the walls may also illustrate apocryphal miracles of the Virgin, to whom the chapel was dedicated.

8 *The nave of St John's church. The lower storey belongs to the late eleventh-century cathedral; the upper storeys are late twelfth century.*

9 *Reconstruction painting of the Dominican friary as it might have appeared in the fifteenth century, with the City Walls in the foreground (T. Morgan).*

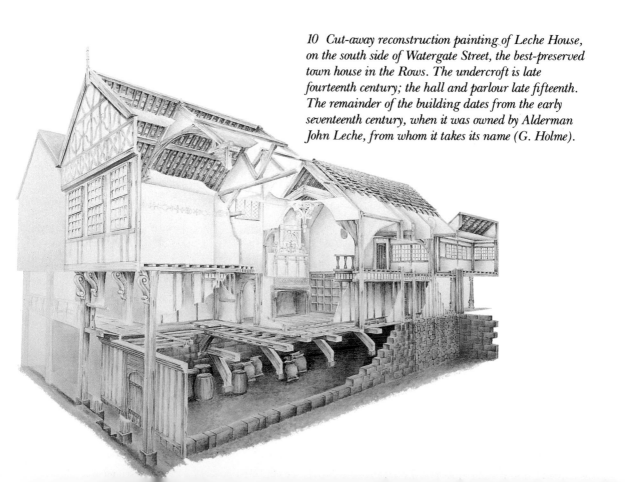

10 *Cut-away reconstruction painting of Leche House, on the south side of Watergate Street, the best-preserved town house in the Rows. The undercroft is late fourteenth century; the hall and parlour late fifteenth. The remainder of the building dates from the early seventeenth century, when it was owned by Alderman John Leche, from whom it takes its name (G. Holme).*

11   Reconstruction painting showing the back of the North Wall being reinforced with soil during the Civil War siege to make it more resistant to artillery bombardment (G. Sumner).

12   Chester Exchange, built in 1695–8 in the Market Square and demolished after a fire in 1862. The single-storey buildings to its south (left) are the Green Market and Fish Market, and to its north (right) the Meat Market; these were replaced by a new Market Hall in 1863. Oil painting by D. Hodgson, 1830 or 1831.

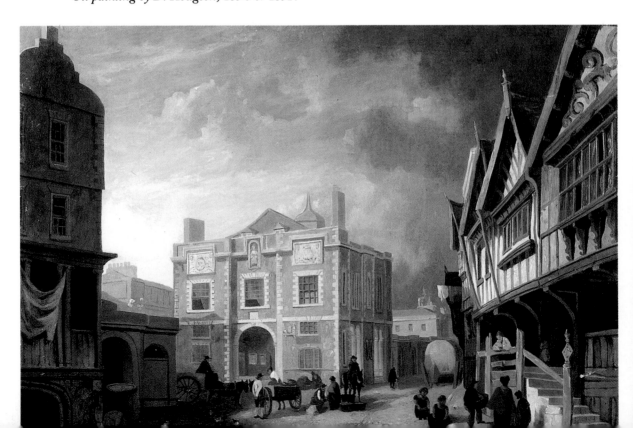

13 Mid-nineteenth century view of Chester from Curzon Park. On the right Harrison's
Grosvenor Bridge, opened in 1832, is visible.

14 Chester Town Hall in a water-colour by
Louise Rayner of about 1880. The low red brick
building to its left was the poultry market.

15 Chester cathedral, now one of the city's most popular tourist attractions.

16 'A Celebration of Chester', bronze statue by Stephen Broadbent unveiled in 1992.

materials. However, Chester seems to have had more of its population involved in the industry than elsewhere: in the late sixteenth and seventeenth centuries it accounted for over a fifth of the craftsmen in the city.

The leather industry consisted of several distinct trades, encompassing the preparation of the leather and its conversion into finished goods. The processing and preparation of the animal skins was divided into the tanning of heavy hides such as those of cattle and horses, and the treating of light skins such as those of sheep, deer, goat and game. Tanning usually entailed soaking the hides in pits containing oak bark and water for a period of up to two years. Prior to tanning, the hides would have received several other treatments, including being soaked in lime to loosen the hair. Curriers finished tanned hides with oil and tallow to make them supple and waterproof. Lighter skins were treated with alum or train oils (oil from whales, seals or various fish). This process would be carried out by skinners, glovers, tawyers or whitawyers. The leather so produced was soft and suitable for clothing and gloves.

The finished leather was then fashioned into objects. This involved a variety of craftsmen, such as shoemakers/cordwainers, saddlers,

glovers, pursers, girdlers, sheath- and scabbard-makers. Some of these craftsmen would have had their own shops where they made and sold their goods; others would have worked from home and sold their wares to middlemen.

The raw hides and skins would mainly have been supplied by the butchers in the city or would have been bought from traders, but skins were also imported from Ireland and the Isle of Man. Sheepskins were the main import, but there are records of goatskins as well as pelts of badger, otter, marten and coney. The trade in furs was an old one, with marten furs being mentioned in Domesday. In the sixteenth and seventeenth centuries Chester glovers would travel to Liverpool, which also imported Irish skins, if they could not buy what they wanted in Chester. Skins were also imported via coastal trade from elsewhere in Britain.

As with many urban tradesmen, the various sections of the leather crafts were organized into guilds. Guilds regulated the activities of craftsmen within the town, ensuring that qual-

55 *'South Prospect of the City of Chester' by John Boydell (1749). Note the skinners' drying sheds by the river. On the right the Outer Bridgegate, the mills and the water tower above the Inner Bridgegate are visible.*

ity and prices were maintained and guarding against unfair trading practices. They probably came into existence at the end of the thirteenth century, but whether the leather trades were officially organized at that time is uncertain, as there is little documentary evidence until the mid-fourteenth century.

Documentary sources increase considerably from the early sixteenth century and show a thriving commercial trade in leather and leather goods. Tradesmen's debtors lists tell us where their customers lived. Shoemakers' customers came mainly from north-western England. Saddlers seem to have sold mainly to people from the Cheshire countryside, but also to a few from Ireland. Glovers had customers throughout the north-west and in Ireland. Many goods would have been bought by people who had come to Chester on business, but the glovers were active in trading. They took their finished goods to London, and Chester, along with Bristol, became known as one of the major suppliers to the London merchants. Large quantities of tanned calf skins, which were the city's main exportable commodity in the sixteenth and seventeenth centuries, were shipped under special licence by Chester merchants. These were sent to the Continent, notably Spain and France, but occasionally cargoes were sent further abroad, such as to Danzig in 1606–7.

Documents and place-names indicate where some businesses were located. In Middle English a shoemaker was called a corviser, and 'Le coruyserrowe' and 'Corvisors' Row' are mentioned in 1356 and 1651 respectively. They are thought to have been situated on the corner of Bridge Street and Eastgate Street. Souters Lane is still in existence today; its name is derived from Old English 'sutere', again meaning a shoemaker. It is not known why the lane was so named, but the cordwainers did have their meeting house in St John's churchyard nearby. Bridge Street may also have been the

site of saddlers' businesses – 'Sadelerisrowe' and 'Sadelesrowe' are recorded in 1342 and 1304 and are thought to have been in Bridge Street near White Friars.

The tanning and preparation of skins was an unpleasant and smelly process. These businesses were therefore often placed on the edge of towns, where they would cause the least offence. Archaeological evidence for late medieval tanning in Chester has been found in Love Street, where about fourteen rectangular pits have been interpreted as tanning pits. Union Street nearby used to be called Barker's Lane and may have been used for deliveries of bark to the tanneries. Tanning continued into the nineteenth century not far away in Queen Street. Both sites are outside the City Walls and not far from the cattle markets at Gorse Stacks. Two tanners are recorded as renting land outside the Bars, one of them on the road to Boughton. However, in the late Saxon period, tanning seems to have been carried on nearer the centre of the town, as tan pits have been found in Lower Bridge Street.

Glovers and skinners had workshops on the western side of the city, between the river and City Walls. An eighteenth-century picture shows the skinners' drying sheds by the water-side (55). An area of land outside the Castle gate was known as the Gloverstone after a large stone which marked the limits of the City Council's jurisdiction. The area was thus a place of refuge from the City's laws, including those controlling trade. A number of glovers lived in the area, and the stone may have derived its name from the fact that it was used as a leather-dressing block.

The leather industry in Chester continued into the nineteenth century, although it had already begun to decline in the early eighteenth with the increase in tanning in Ireland, the removal of protective legislation and to some extent a greater emphasis on dairy farming, which led to fewer hides being available locally.

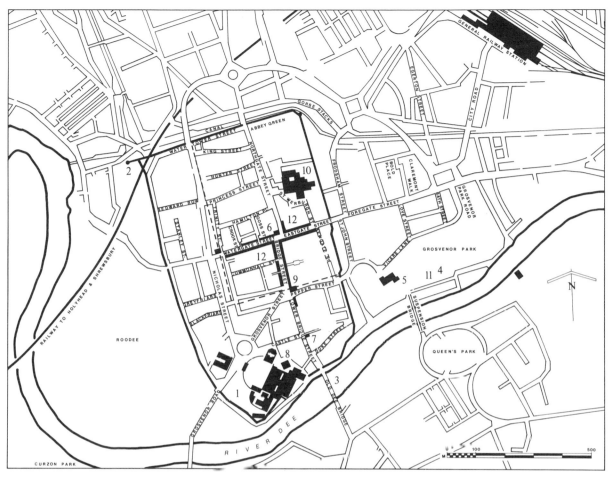

56 *Map of present-day Chester showing the location of visible medieval remains.*

1 *The Castle motte, Agricola Tower and Flag Tower*
2 *The City Walls, including Spur Wall and Water Tower*
3 *The Old Dee Bridge*
4 *The Shipgate (re-erected in the Grosvenor Park)*
5 *St John's Church and ruins*
6 *St Peter's Church*
7 *St Olave's Church*
8 *St Mary's Church*
9 *St Michael's Church (now Chester City Council Heritage Centre)*
10 *Cathedral*
11 *Chancel arch of St Mary's Nunnery (re-erected in the Grosvenor Park)*
12 *The Rows and crypts – Watergate Street, Bridge Street, Eastgate Street, Northgate Street*

6

The Civil War Siege

Background

The breakdown in relations between King Charles I and Parliament which led to the Civil War was a long process with several causes and a considerable sense of grievance had built up, especially among what would now be termed the middle classes. Matters came to a head in 1640 when the king's attempt to impose a new prayer book on Scotland resulted in open rebellion. This was followed by a revolt in Ireland. The king had troops there under his Lord Lieutenant, the Earl of Ormonde, but more were clearly needed. Both the king and Parliament wanted command of these troops to ensure their own safety. Through the summer of 1642, both sides started to raise troops and the country became split into two factions.

In general terms, London and the south and east sided with Parliament. The more traditional areas of the north, Wales and the south-west declared for the king. The important military magazines, Portsmouth and Kingston-upon-Hull, as well as the Tower of London and the navy, were held for Parliament. Religion was also a significant factor. The Parliamentarian side became identified with the new independent Protestant movements, the Royalists with the traditional Church of England and the Roman Catholics. The nature of the split meant that in the long run it would be very difficult for the king to win militarily; his best hope was therefore to achieve a quick victory. Throughout the war Chester was close

to the front line. The small number of influential families who effectively controlled the city sided with the king, a feeling which by and large appears to have been reflected by the citizens as a whole.

The outbreak of the war

On 8 August 1642, Sir William Brereton, MP for Cheshire, attempted to raise troops in the city for Parliament. He was surrounded by a hostile crowd and taken into custody by the Mayor, Thomas Cowper, for his own safety and ejected from the city the following morning.

King Charles raised the royal standard at Nottingham on 22 August. From 23 to 28 September he was entertained at Chester by the Mayor and Corporation. Chester was an important place to secure because at this time it was still the main port for Ireland, where the king had loyal troops. Several regiments of soldiers were raised in Cheshire to serve in the king's army.

It was generally hoped that the struggle between the king and Parliament would be quickly settled. However, the first major battle at Edgehill in Warwickshire was inconclusive, and the nation prepared for a long conflict.

The Civil War around Chester only really started early in 1643, when Brereton returned from London with a commission as the Parliamentary commander for Cheshire (**57**). The history of the ensuing siege of Chester can be split into four phases.

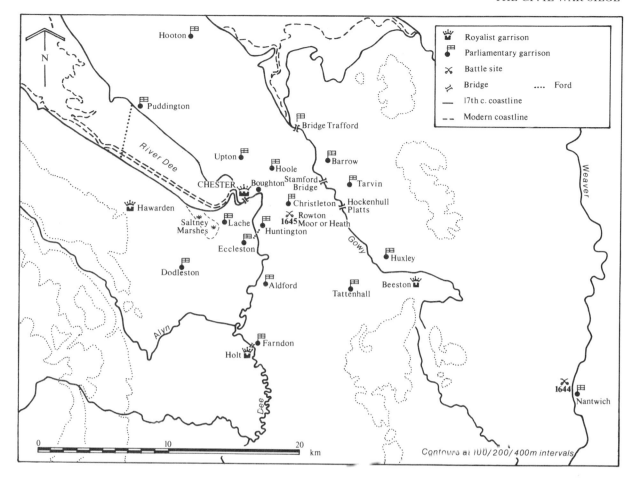

Phase 1: January 1643–March 1644

Brereton established his headquarters at Nantwich and started to raise troops. The king sent Colonel Ellis, a professional soldier, to supervise the construction of defence works at Chester. He designed an extensive system of earthen ramparts with gun mounts to defend the suburbs outside the City Walls (**58**).

During the summer of 1643, Brereton established his control over Cheshire. No doubt the local Royalist commanders were missing the regiments that had been sent to join the king. During July the first attack was made against the city, when the Parliamentary forces raided the outworks. As a precaution, the citizens razed Boughton to the ground. By November 1643, Brereton was ready to move all his forces against Chester. He invaded North Wales and seized Hawarden Castle, intending to sever the

57 *Disposition of military forces in Cheshire during the Civil War.*

city's supply lines. His progress was cut short, however, by the arrival of several thousand troops from the king's army in Ireland, and he was forced to retire to his main garrisons.

With new troops and a new governor, Lord Byron, sent by the king, the Royalists went on to the offensive. On 13 December a small party of soldiers scaled the crags of Beeston Castle and seized it from the Parliamentary governor. The loss of this stronghold, in a strategic position between Chester and Nantwich, was a serious blow to the Parliamentarians, and the governor was executed soon afterwards.

In bitter winter weather, the Royalist army started to assault Nantwich. Brereton and his cavalry escaped and organized a relief force.

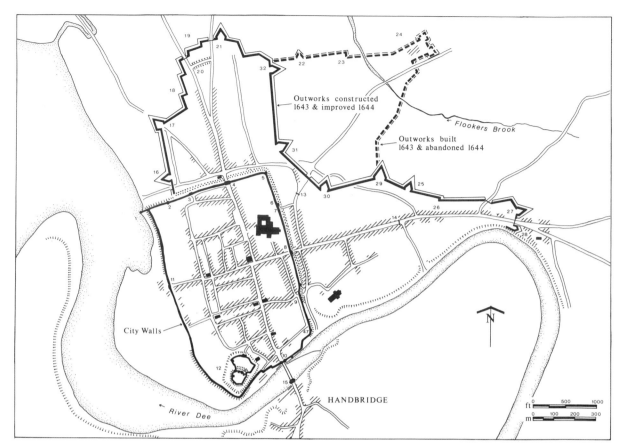

58 *Chester: medieval defences and Royalist outworks held 1643/4. (The smaller numbers have no significance.)*

Joined by the cavalry of the Northern Association under Sir Thomas Fairfax, he defeated Byron's army on 25 January at the Battle of Nantwich.

Phase 2: March 1644–November 1644
Early in 1644, the situation in the north had become critical for the king. Not only had the Irish and Chester forces been heavily defeated at Nantwich, but a Scottish army had entered the war on the side of Parliament. They had seized Newcastle and were besieging York. To restore the situation, the king sent an army to Chester under his brilliant young nephew, Prince Rupert. He arrived on 11 March.

Prince Rupert inspected the defences and gave directions for their improvement (**colour plate 11**). The outworks were shortened and raised. For the next five months, the prince made Chester his base. From here he raised the siege of Newark in Nottinghamshire, cam-

paigned in south Lancashire and captured Liverpool. Finally, in late June he marched his army to the relief of York. On 2 July he fought the combined Parliamentary and Scottish army at Marston Moor, close to York. The result was a complete defeat for the Royalists. York fell, and Prince Rupert returned to Chester with his shattered army. In August he retired south to the king's headquarters at Oxford.

Phase 3: November 1644–September 1645
At this time Chester suffered its first serious siege. Brereton established a forward headquarters at Tarvin and placed garrisons in the villages surrounding the city. He also started to besiege Beeston Castle and put a force into Hawarden to watch the castle there with the intention of cutting Chester off from its sources

86

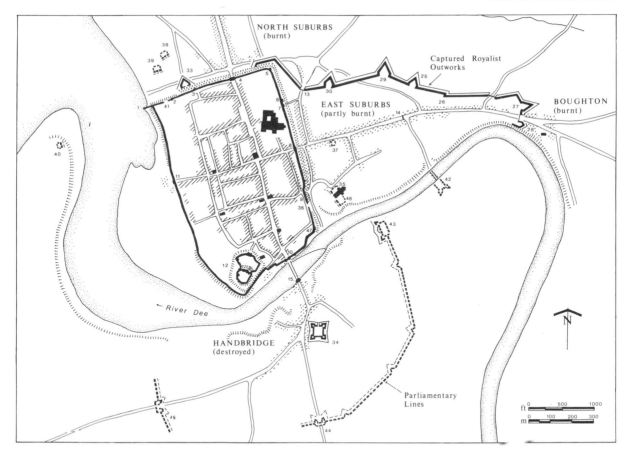

59 *Chester: medieval defences, Royalist outworks held 1645 and Parliamentary siegeworks 1645/6.*

of supply. On 18 January 1645, Byron mounted a raid from the city against the garrison at Christleton. Brereton's efficient intelligence system gave him prior warning and he ambushed the raid and beat it back to the city. He followed this up with raids against the city's outworks, but these were driven off.

The situation was considered critical enough for a further relief force to be sent by the king. On 19 February Prince Maurice (Rupert's younger brother) arrived with an army, forcing Brereton to withdraw his forces. Maurice inspected the outworks and again recommended that they be shortened because of the difficulty of manning them (**59**). The Northgate suburbs were abandoned and burnt, along with Great Boughton and Christleton. Morgan's Mount was built to defend the North Wall.

After a month, Maurice left and the siege was resumed. By early May, Chester, Hawarden Castle and Beeston Castle were all placed under tighter siege.

Meanwhile, the king had left Oxford with his main army and was moving northwards. By May he reached the southern border of Cheshire. Brereton was concerned that his forces might be caught by the king while dispersed among his various garrisons. Consequently, he withdrew all his forces from the western or Welsh side of the Dee. Believing that this meant that the siege was effectively lifted, the king turned his army eastwards into the Midlands. Eventually, on 14 June, he met the Parliamentary New Model Army under Fairfax and Cromwell at Naseby in Northamptonshire and was completely defeated.

The siege of Chester was not immediately resumed, however. Brereton was caught by the provisions of the Self-Denying Ordinance, whereby a Member of Parliament could not also serve as a military commander. He was obliged to go down to London, and the war in Chester was pursued with much less vigour in his absence. Byron used this opportunity to build a substantial fort in Handbridge.

Phase 4: September 1645–February 1646

On the night of the 20 September the Parliamentarians launched a well-laid plan to storm the outworks. They surprised the guard at Boughton, opened the gates and poured into the eastern suburbs. Though initially taken aback, the defenders managed to close the Eastgate and resist attempts to take the whole city. From that time until the end of the siege, the defenders held only the old City Walls, Morgan's Mount and the Royal Fort in Handbridge.

The Parliamentarians brought up cannon to St John's churchyard and battered a breach in the City Walls by the Newgate. The attempt to storm the breach on 22 September was driven back after fierce fighting. Hearing of the city's plight, King Charles, who was in North Wales, marched with a force of cavalry to Chester, arriving on 23 September. The following day his cavalry were routed by a force under Colonel Poyntz at Rowton Moor, 5km (3 miles) south-east of Chester. The day afterwards, King Charles departed and the siege resumed.

The Parliamentarians brought up more cannon, and in October another breach was battered in the North Wall near the Water Tower. Again the defenders drove back the attempts to storm these breaches. The attackers then changed their tactics and instituted a policy of bombardment and close blockade. At the end of October Brereton returned to take command of the Parliamentary forces.

The remainder of the siege was marked by the bombardment of the city. Numerous houses, the mills and St Peter's Church were severely damaged. To link the attacking forces on either side of the river, a bridge of boats was constructed upstream of Chester. Several sallies were made by the besieged. The most notable was on 21 November, when two fire boats were launched on an exceptionally high tide against the bridge of boats. An attack was made simultaneously on the Parliamentary positions on the southern side of the river.

These various efforts proved ineffectual. By the end of January 1646 the city's position had become critical, and it was apparent that the king's cause was doomed. Negotiations were opened and on 3 February the city surrendered to the Parliamentary forces. The garrison was allowed to march out to Conwy Castle.

The aftermath

Following the surrender, the Royalists were displaced from public office and replaced by Parliamentarians. Many had to pay fines for 'delinquency', that is for supporting the king. The city had been badly damaged during the siege: the suburbs of Spital, Boughton, Christleton and Handbridge had been destroyed, together with many houses in Foregate Street, Cow Lane, St John's Lane, outside the Northgate and outside the Watergate. Within the City Walls most of the buildings in Eastgate Street and halfway down Watergate Street had been damaged by the bombardment. The City's silver plate had been melted down for coin. The normal markets and economic life had been totally disrupted. The occupying soldiers pulled down the High Cross at the centre of the city outside St Peter's and ransacked the Bishop's Palace adjacent to the Cathedral.

Civil War remains

The effects of the Civil War can be observed in several places on the City Walls. At the start of the War, the Corporation undertook various measures to bring the Walls up to a defensible standard. The Spur Wall to the Water Tower has battlements that have been converted to gun ports for cannon and the War seems the most probable occasion for this modification. Some traces of the damage suffered are also visible. On the tower near the south-eastern angle of the Walls the marks left by cannon balls can still be seen, and near the Newgate, the filled-in breach made by the attackers can be identified (**60**). Finally, the tower at the north-eastern corner of the Walls will always be associated with King Charles. Formerly known as the Phoenix Tower, it now bears his name, as it was from the roof of this tower that he observed part of the battle of Rowton Moor.

Of the extensive outworks that were built to defend the suburbs, virtually nothing survives as they have been swallowed up under more recent developments. However, their course and history can be reconstructed from the accounts written at the time. To protect the North Wall, Morgan's Mount was constructed

just outside the Wall to contain a large cannon. It was probably a free-standing angular earthwork. Nowadays the name has been transferred to the square stone tower which projects forward of the City Walls at this point. A 'great trench' was also cut between Parkgate and Liverpool Road to facilitate the transfer of guns between the mounts; this exists today as Rock Lane.

After the Parliamentarians captured the eastern outworks in September 1645, they erected various works, but again little has survived the recent growth of the city. Their works were probably much slighter than those of the Royalists and would have made much use of timber and debris from demolished buildings. The main force in the eastern suburbs could, of course, reuse the captured earthworks. Banks were built to defend the gun batteries set up to attack the North Wall. The guns in St John's churchyard probably made use of its surrounding wall. The end of the bridge of boats

60 *The City Walls in the 'Roman Gardens' south of the Newgate. The unweathered stonework in the middle of the picture fills the breach battered in the Walls by Parliamentary cannon located in St John's churchyard.*

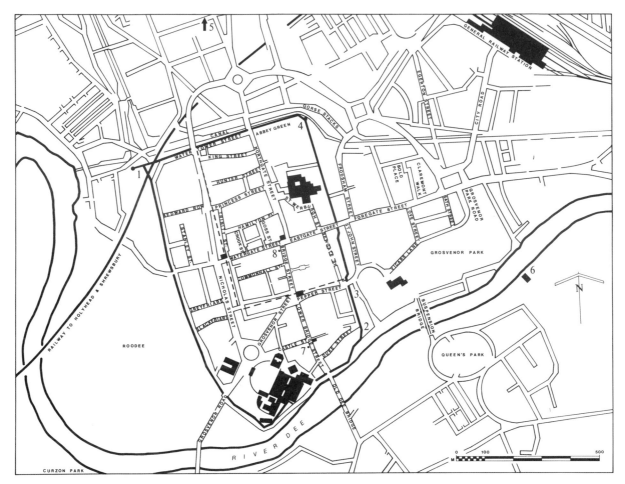

was protected by the Lower Mount built on the Meadows. A low rectangular earthwork still survives in this position and is thought to be the only visible survivor of the Parliamentary siegeworks.

Numerous buildings in the city have associations with the Civil War. Gamul House in Lower Bridge Street was the home of Sir Francis Gamul. Here King Charles stayed during his visit in 1645. Cowper House at 12 Bridge Street was the home of Thomas Cowper, mayor in 1642. It still bears the initials TC carved on a beam across its frontage.

61 *Map of present-day Chester showing the location of visible Civil War remains.*

1 *Gun embrasures in Spur Wall*
2 *Cannonball marks on tower at south-eastern corner of the City Walls*
3 *Repaired breach in the City Walls (visible from the Roman Gardens)*
4 *King Charles' Tower*
5 *Rock Lane*
6 *Earthworks of the Parliamentary 'Lower Mount' (visible among the trees just past the school boat-house)*
7 *Gamul House*
8 *Copwer House*

7

Restoration Chester

Chester had been devastated by the effects of the Civil War and its citizens had suffered many hardships for their loyalty to the king. The horrors of the long siege remained in people's memories for many years, and the scars of the war were visible throughout the city for decades, with the gaps of devastated buildings yawning in the main streets. The population which had suffered death, injury and starvation during the siege had been further weakened by the plague. Almost twenty percent of the total population is thought to have been wiped out during a major epidemic in 1647.

Nevertheless, the years of Interregnum (1646–60) do not appear to have been too unkind. After an uncertain start, Chester enjoyed good relations with the major-generals. The City Corporation gradually began to reassert its authority and attempts by central government to curb its power were resisted. Normal social conditions began to be restored. The city's trade, decimated by the siege, started to revive.

The restoration of the monarchy in May 1660 was generally welcomed by the people of Chester. The Corporation swiftly declared its loyalty to the Crown and addresses of laudation and congratulation were sent to the new king, Charles II, and the Cathedral was restored to its former status and use.

Trade and industry

Chester's markets and fairs gradually regained their regional importance, so that by the end of the century the city was the major wholesaling and retailing market for Cheshire and North Wales. The weekly markets, controlled by the City Corporation, increasingly dealt in luxury goods as well as local produce. Markets for bread, vegetables, fish, dairy produce, meat and poultry were held in Northgate Street, and there were also poultry, cheese and butter markets in Bridge Street. Flax and linen markets were held in Eastgate Row North until the early eighteenth century.

The two annual fairs, held at Midsummer and Michaelmas, each lasted about fifteen days. They provided the only opportunity for those who were not freemen of the city to trade. For the rest of the year, the city guilds continued to monopolize trade and fiercely resisted outside competition. Merchants from a wide area flocked into Chester during the fairs, increasingly trading in manufactured as well as agricultural goods.

Flour production was monopolized by the corn mills at the Dee Bridge. In the seventeenth century there were eleven waterwheels at work: six for grinding corn, three for fulling cloth and two for raising water. There were also extensive fulling mills on the southern side of the weir in Handbridge. The city's water supply was raised from the Dee to a water tower on the Bridgegate and then piped to properties in the city. Another water tower at Spital in Boughton supplied water to a conduit at the Cross.

Chester's industrial base continued to depend

on the traditional leather trade. Some new industries did develop after the Restoration, but these seem to have been relatively small-scale. They included tobacco and snuff manufacture, pipe-making and felt-hat making. Shipbuilding was established by the end of the century and there was a shipyard on the Roodee. A royal mint for silver coins was established briefly in 1696 making machine-pressed half crowns.

The port

The port recovered rapidly after the Civil War, largely because of improved economic conditions in Ireland. Indeed, the Irish trade was to become the life-blood of the port throughout the later seventeenth century, far exceeding that with the Continent. Exports included manufactured goods, Cheshire salt, and coal and metals from North Wales. The major imports were hides for the tanning industry, linen and linen cloth. The linen trade became increasingly important with over 60,000 yards of linen passing through the port by 1700.

Chester's coasting trade also expanded at this time, with larger vessels visiting more destinations. The main cargoes were coal, cheese and lead. However, foreign trade enjoyed mixed fortunes, largely due to the disruptions caused by wars in Europe. The traditional export of tanned calf skins declined, but there was a large increase in the export of pig lead and lead ore to the Low Countries. Imports included Spanish and Portuguese wines and timber, and flax and hemp from the Baltic and Scandinavia. There was a small tobacco and cotton trade with North America.

By the end of the century the port of Chester was prospering, but fears for its future remained. The ancient problem of the silting of the Dee estuary and channel persisted. Parkgate replaced Neston as the main outport during the late seventeenth century, and soon became the main embarkation point for Ireland as well as a fashionable sea-bathing resort. There were

62 *The 'Bear and Billet' in Lower Bridge Street, the most impressive of the new timber-framed town houses built after the Civil War.*

a number of proposals to make the river navigable to Chester for larger vessels, but it was not until 1699 that an Act of Parliament to authorize such work was obtained and this was only of limited success.

Reconstruction

Growing economic prosperity was reflected in the amount of new building which took place after the Restoration. In part this was due to the continued reconstruction of buildings damaged or destroyed during the Civil War, but there was also considerable new building work in accordance with changing social patterns and architectural taste.

The destruction suffered by the city during the siege took many years to make good. Rebuilding seems to have been slow to start and continued throughout the 1650s and well into the 1660s. Some of Chester's best known timber buildings date from this time. They include the 'Bear and Billet' in Lower Bridge Street, a new town house built in 1664 for the Earl of Shrewsbury, almost certainly to replace one destroyed during the siege (**62**). In the same year, Thomas Cowper, the former Royalist Mayor of Chester, improved his house at 12 Bridge Street, which had probably been damaged during the hostilities.

During this period of post-war rebuilding, timber continued to be used for even the most important houses. Supplies were plentiful and cheap, and so the local tradition of timber-framing lasted well into the later seventeenth century. However, new architectural styles were already becoming fashionable. After the

Restoration, classical architectural forms gradually spread to the provinces, transforming regional vernacular styles. The Great Fire of London of 1666 had an equally profound effect on the construction and design of town houses. In Chester, as in other towns, new building began to be regulated in an effort to reduce the dangers of fire. Bricks, which had never been widely used in the area before the Civil War, were now manufactured in large numbers. By 1680 there was a substantial brickworks on Hough Green, south of the river (**63**).

During the last two decades of the seventeenth century, there was considerable building activity, as Chester's wealthiest citizens replaced their old timber houses with elegant brick mansions (**64**). This process was most marked in the fashionable Lower Bridge Street area, where many of the local gentry owned substantial properties. Some original houses were simply encased or re-fronted in brick: for

63 *Brickmaking on Edgar's Field, south of the river Dee in Handbridge.*

example, the medieval great hall of Gamul House in Lower Bridge Street is concealed behind a late seventeenth-century facade.

Whenever houses were rebuilt, the owners tried to take the opportunity to enclose the Rows passing through the front of their properties. Rows were essentially medieval structures; curiosities which were no longer compatible with current architectural taste. Contemporary commentators described them as ugly and old

64 *Late seventeenth-century houses at 15 and 17 Castle Street. The steep gables surmounted by finials pre-date later classical influences.*

fashioned. Celia Fiennes, who visited Chester in 1698, thought that they 'darken the streetes and hinder the light of the houses in many places'. People wishing to get rid of their Rows argued that their new houses would be a considerable improvement to the street. In a typical petition of 1676, Lady Mary Calveley requested permission to take down her house in Lower Bridge Street '...and to rebuild the same roe as may bee a grace and ornament to the city'.

This petition, like those of many of her neighbours, was granted by the City Assembly. Lady Mary Calveley was fined a substantial sum of £20 for the loss of the Row, but was permitted to build the fine Baroque mansion known as Bridge House (now the Oddfellows Hall). While the City Assembly continued to resist Row enclosures in other parts of the city, they put up little resistance in Lower Bridge Street. Over the next century the Rows there disappeared with one exception on the eastern side of the street. Lower Bridge Street was some distance from the city centre and the loss of the Rows here may have been considered less important than elsewhere in Chester. However, the members of the Assembly probably accepted the pressures for architectural change which motivated so many of Chester's leading citizens to rebuild and remodel their houses at this time.

Indeed, the Assembly itself embarked on a programme of rebuilding which was to continue well into the eighteenth century. A new Common Hall or Exchange was built between 1695 and 1698 on the site of the old Shambles in Northgate Street. It replaced the Common Hall of Pleas housed in the medieval chapel of St Nicholas. Built in brick with stone quoins, the Exchange was much admired, described by one visitor as 'the best piece of building' in the city (**colour plate 12**). The upper floors were used by the Assembly for meetings, courts and social functions. A gilded statue of Queen Anne in her coronation robes was added to the south front following her accession in 1702.

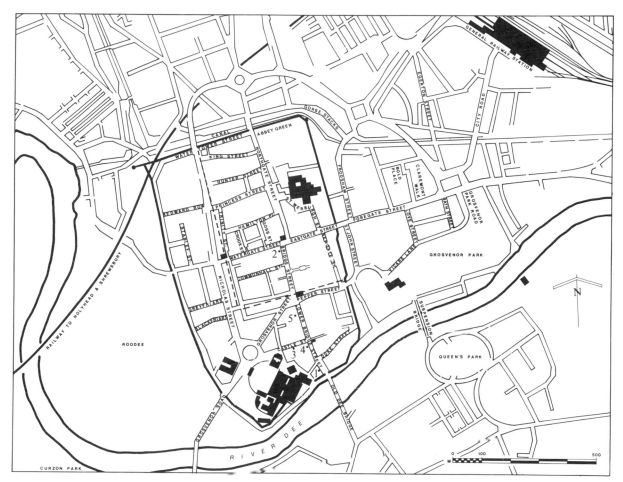

65 *Map of present day Chester showing the location of*
Restoration buildings.

1 *The 'Bear and Billet'*
2 *Cowper House*
3 *15 & 17 Castle Street*
4 *Gamul House*
5 *Oddfellows' Hall*

8

Georgian and Regency Chester

Chester was typical of many other Georgian county towns: prosperous, expanding, confident and fashionable. Besides being the centre of county administration, judiciary and politics, it was a garrison town, cathedral city and the main retailing centre for the surrounding region. It also flourished as a social centre for the leisured gentry and professional classes, who gravitated to the city for company, entertainment and pleasure. To cater for their increasingly sophisticated needs, Georgian Chester became a centre of skills and craftsmanship, providing the luxury goods and quality services which polite society now required.

Chester grew steadily in size and population during the eighteenth century. The population rose from about 9000 at the beginning of the century to just over 15,000 in 1801. The physician Dr Haygarth attributed this relatively low growth rate to 'the want of manufactures, which might enable the lower classes to marry in early youth'. However, there was a sharp increase in the first thirty years of the nineteenth century, when the population rose by more than one third to over 21,000 in 1831.

At the beginning of this period most people still lived within the City Walls, with only small areas of development beyond the Northgate, along Foregate Street and in the suburbs of Handbridge and Boughton. There were still many open spaces behind the main streets, and west of Nicholas Street a large open area of fields and gardens stretched back to the Walls.

Regency Chester was a very different place. There had been a great expansion of building inside the Walls: gardens and vacant plots had been infilled with clusters of small houses behind the principal streets. New housing and industries had grown up, particularly to the north of Foregate Street beside the new Chester Canal. The open land on the western side of the city had almost disappeared.

Trade and industry
Chester's economic prosperity during this period was largely due to its role as a retailing and servicing centre. Traditional industries, such as ship-building, leather-working and glove- and snuff-manufacture all declined and were not replaced. By the early nineteenth century, Chester's only heavy industries were a foundry in Charles Street and two leadworks: one in Commonhall Street and the other, which operated until recently, to the north of the canal on the eastern side of the city.

Instead, Chester developed a diverse economy. By the 1780s the population was employed in over one hundred separate trades and crafts, with the emphasis on high standards of skill and workmanship. The city became noted for its clockmakers, silversmiths, pewterers and cutlers. During this period there was a marked increase in the number of shops offering specialist goods and services, including wine and spirit dealers, hatters, mercers and drapers, perriwig makers and booksellers. By 1784 there

66 *The 'Pied Bull' in Northgate Street, one of Chester's leading eighteenth-century coaching inns.*

were at least sixteen hairdressers in Chester.

Chester's markets and fairs remained an important feature of commercial life until the end of the eighteenth century. The Michaelmas and Midsummer fairs attracted wholesalers and retailers from all over the country, trading in clothing, textiles and manufactured goods. Hop fairs were held in large warehouses behind the Blossoms and Hop Pole inns in Foregate Street.

Coaching

Chester's continuing commercial success was greatly assisted by improvements in transport. Until Telford's new road between Shrewsbury and Holyhead opened in 1830, Chester was an important coaching centre for passengers to and from Ireland. Both Handel and Jonathan Swift stayed in Chester. Dean Swift was so appalled by the poor road conditions and

uncomfortable springless carriages that he was moved to write:

> When soon by every hillock rut and stone,
> In each other's faces by turns were thrown . . .
> Sweet Company! Next time, I do protest, Sir,
> I'd walk to Dublin ere I'd ride to Chester.

However, the development of an efficient turnpike road system and improvements in coach design meant that there was a rapid expansion of coaching services from Chester. By the middle of the eighteenth century, there were well over fifty coaches leaving the city each week and the journey to London took only two days. Coaching services were controlled by a small number of inn proprietors, mainly grouped around the market place. The most famous coaching inn, the White Lion, was demolished in the 1860s, but the Pied Bull in Northgate Street still survives (**66**).

By the early nineteenth century, services had so proliferated that coaches could not manoeuvre in the crowded market place. The Golden Lion in Foregate Street and the Feathers in Bridge Street became the principal coaching inns. There was a notable rise in services to North Wales, evidence that Chester was beginning to develop as a tourist centre.

The port and canals

Chester's port prospered in the early eighteenth century. However, the old problem of the silting of the Dee continued to cause concern. In 1731, despite strong opposition, the Corporation accepted a proposal to make the Dee navigable from the sea to Chester for ships of 200 tons by digging a channel to achieve a depth of 16 feet of water at moderate spring tide. An Act of Parliament was obtained in 1732 and the channel was dug in 1735–6 and a new quay was built at Crane Wharf (**67**). In 1740 the River Dee Company was incorporated to recover and preserve the navigation. Although the company reclaimed several thousand acres of marshland in the Dee estuary, there were frequent complaints that it failed in its statutory obligation to improve the channel. Neverthe-less, trade remained steady throughout the eighteenth century and any decline was only relative to the meteoric rise of the port of Liverpool, which had established its supremacy by the end of the century.

In the 1770s canals seemed to offer a new prospect of prosperity. A proposal to build a canal to link the Dee with the new Trent and Mersey Canal at Middlewich was enthusiast-ically supported in the hope that this would attract some of the trade from Liverpool and the Midlands. Work started in 1772, but the Trent and Mersey company refused to allow the new canal to be joined to their system, fearing loss of trade to Chester. Instead the Chester Canal Company constructed a 25-km (16-mile) long canal to Nantwich in the heart of agricultural Cheshire, finished in 1779. However, the canal was not connected to the national network and by 1790 it had fallen into disuse.

Already a new scheme was being proposed for a waterway which would link Montgomery-shire and the Wrexham iron-making district to the river Mersey, making use of the Chester Canal for part of its route. Work on the new Ellesmere Canal began in 1793. By 1797, Chester had been linked with the river Mersey at Ellesmere Port. A new canal basin was built at Tower Wharf, with warehouses, dry dock, iron roving-bridge and a canal tavern. The new canal was a success and established Chester as an important canal port. The passenger trade between Chester and Liverpool was immediately popular; the journey by packet boat took just three hours. The fortunes of the old Chester Canal were restored and new industry and commerce grew up along its banks. In 1833, exactly 61 years after the first sod of the Chester Canal had been cut, a link was made with the Trent and Mersey Canal at Middlewich.

Social life

During the early years of the eighteenth century Chester became the occasional residence of many country gentry who left their rural estates to live in their town houses for the winter months. It also attracted a powerful nucleus of resident city gentry. The gentry, together with the rising professional classes, demanded an active social life, and Georgian Chester came to provide many sophisticated and fashionable entertainments for a growing population with the wealth and leisure to enjoy them.

The city developed a well-established winter social season with a continual round of assemblies, card evenings and theatrical performances. Its climax was the spring race meeting in the first week of May, when large numbers flocked into Chester, staying in the principal inns or privately-rented houses. The presence of so many resident gentry and professional families ensured that social and cultural gatherings continued throughout the year, with regular concerts, balls, lectures and cultural activities.

New facilities were provided to cater for the demands of fashionable society. The Exchange in Northgate Street, completed in 1698, included an Assembly Room, a coffee-house and a subscription library. However, the demand for larger and more elegant surroundings led to the conversion of Booth Mansion, Watergate Street, into another assembly room in the 1740s. It was not until 1777, when new rooms were built by public subscription at the Talbot Inn in Eastgate Street, that Chester gained purpose-built assembly rooms which could rival those in other leading provincial towns. The Talbot, rebuilt on a lavish scale as the Royal Hotel in 1785, became the social centre of Chester.

Although Roger Comberbache, Clerk to the Pentice, records watching plays in 1692,

67 *Crane Wharf was developed after the canalization of the Dee in the 1730s. The wharves and warehouses shown in this cartouche of 1772 still survive.*

Chester did not gain a purpose-built theatre until 1773, when the medieval St Nicholas' chapel in Northgate Street was reconstructed as the New Theatre, later the Theatre Royal. All the famous actors of the day, including Sarah Siddons and Edmund Kean, played in Chester, where they were received by the most distinguished families and were mobbed by admiring crowds.

This expansion in the city's social life was reflected in new opportunities for personal display. A riverside walk known as The Groves was laid out in 1732. Another popular promenade was through the Cherry Orchards at Boughton 'whose pleasant walks and Arbours entice a Number of People in the Summer Time'. For lovers of sport there were three bowling greens and the city cock-pit, situated between Park Street and Souters Lane. In 1818 two acres of park land behind the Albion Hotel in Lower Bridge Street were converted to public pleasure gardens with lawns, extensive flower gardens and a bowling green.

Architecture

For a family to enjoy this new social life, it had to have an appropriate town house. From the end of the seventeenth century, many of Chester's old timber buildings were rebuilt or remodelled in the new classical styles. The rebuilding and consequent loss of the Rows in Lower Bridge Street has already been noted (p. 94). However, Lower Bridge Street was unusual in that a number of completely new houses were built. Elsewhere in the Row system, older properties were encased or refronted in brick, allowing the Row to be preserved in front of the building. For example, in 1700 George Booth, prothonotary and clerk to the Crown for Chester, converted two medieval dwellings in Watergate Street into 'one commodious house'. His imposing new house, one of the finest in Chester, retained much of the original medieval fabric including the Row.

Even so, the process of Row enclosure continued for much of the eighteenth century, those parts furthest from the city centre being the most susceptible. Sections of Row were lost from all four main streets. Today, a number of Chester's eighteenth-century houses have their entrances at first-floor level, indicating that they once contained Rows.

Later Georgian town houses tended to be built outside the City Walls, where the air was thought to be more wholesome and there was room for spacious gardens and outbuildings. Dee House and St John's Rectory in Vicar's Lane and the former Bishop's Palace overlooking the Groves are all handsome brick properties of the mid-eighteenth century. Forest House in Foregate Street, built for the Barnston family in 1759, was possibly the finest Georgian house in Chester. Severely classical, and enclosed behind tall iron railings, it was not widely admired at the time; the nineteenth-century historian Hemingway compared its appearance to a public hospital. The main block in Love Street survives, although heavily altered and used as a night club.

By the mid-eighteenth century, information about the new architectural styles and techniques was widely available. Pattern books from London rapidly disseminated the ideas of leading architects in the provinces and even the most humble jobbing builder now had a text book for guidance. Medieval lanes like White Friars and King Street were rebuilt with modest town houses for the city gentry and professional classes.

New areas of housing were also developed. In the 1750s the cathedral authorities redeveloped part of the abbey precinct, building elegant 'rows of genteel houses in the London style'. The formal but slightly provincial brick terraces on the northern and western sides of Abbey Square were built between 1754 and 1761 around a central green enclosed by iron palisading. A stone column, removed from the Exchange during major alterations in 1756, was erected as an obelisk in the centre of the green. Similar developments to the west of the city were made possible by the prosperity of

the port and Chester's Irish linen trade. Stanley Place was built in the early 1780s as a speculative venture by the proprietors of the Irish Linen Hall. Nicholas Street was built up at the same time. This terrace was occupied by many doctors and became known as 'Pill-box Promenade'. These two spacious developments stood on parts of the large blocks of land that had been occupied by the Franciscan and Dominican friaries respectively and had been under-used since the Dissolution almost two and a half centuries earlier.

Public buildings

The spirit of enlightenment which characterized the Georgian era was reflected in new public buildings. Chester's first charity school was the Blue Coat Hospital, established by public subscription by Bishop Nicholas Stratford in 1700. The surviving building in Northgate Street was erected between 1714 and 1717 but remodelled in the 1850s (**68**). A statue of a Blue Coat boy, wearing his distinctive uniform, stands over the central entrance.

Originally, boys were admitted as boarders only, but in 1783 day-boys or 'green caps' were introduced. They were taught reading, writing and accounts. A Blue Girls School opened in 1720, probably in the same premises, although by 1810 it had moved to new premises in St Martin's-in-the-Fields. The girls were 'instructed in religious and moral duties', reading and writing and basic domestic skills such as sewing, knitting and spinning. The girls' school lasted until 1940 and the Blue Coat School closed in 1949.

Another charitable institution was the General Infirmary, which opened in 1755 in the upper part of the Blue Coat Hospital. In 1761 a substantial new building with beds for one hundred patients was opened in St Martin's-in-the-Fields. It was supported by subscriptions and donations. Sick poor from Chester, Cheshire and North Wales could be admitted upon the recommendation of a subscriber to the Infirmary. For its time the Chester

68 *The Blue Coat Hospital, Upper Northgate Street.*

Infirmary was humane and progressive. Under the direction of the physician Dr John Haygarth, appointed in 1767, it gained the first isolation ward in the country. Part of the original building survives facing City Walls Road.

Churches

Following the Toleration Act of 1689 many nonconformist places of worship were erected in the city, but few have survived. The earliest is thought to have been Matthew Henry's chapel, built 1699–1700 between Crook Street and Trinity Lane. It was demolished in the 1960s. The first Methodist chapel, the Octagon near the Bars, was lost in Victorian times. John Wesley, a frequent visitor to Chester, preached there just after it opened in 1765. In 1812 the Wesleyan Methodists moved to a new chapel in St John Street, which is still in use. Part of

the classical interior survives, but the exterior was rebuilt in 1906.

One of the best mid-eighteenth-century chapels was the Queen Street Congregational Chapel of 1777. Part of the facade has now been incorporated into a new development. At the very end of the Georgian period, the Methodist New Connexion built an imposing neo-classical chapel in Pepper Street. During the present century, it was encased within a garage showroom and only 'rediscovered' during alterations in the mid-1980s. The exposed frontage is now part of a large retail store.

Two new Anglican churches were built in the early nineteenth century: a replacement for the medieval St Bridget's at the corner of Grosvenor Street and Nicholas Street (1828) and St Paul's at Boughton (1830). Neither survived the late Victorian distaste for classical churches. St Paul's was replaced by a picturesque timber structure in the 1870s. St Bridget's, which was thought to have '...none of the characteristics of a Christian Church; and might easily be mistaken for some pagan temple...', was demolished in 1892.

The City Walls and gates

During the course of the eighteenth century there were major changes to Chester's City Walls. During the reign of Queen Anne (1702–14), the Corporation began to repair the walls and convert them into a promenade. However, the Jacobite rebellion of 1745 proved that the defensive role of the Walls was not quite over: the Watergate, Northgate and sallyports were blocked up and several buildings adjoining the

Walls were pulled down. Alterations continued later in the century, when medieval defensive towers such as Saddler's Tower and the Goblin Tower were demolished or removed for the convenience of walkers. The four medieval gateways were taken down and replaced by ornamental bridges: Eastgate (1768–69); Watergate (1778); Bridgegate (1782) (**69**) and Northgate (1810).

The last medieval gate to be demolished, the Northgate, housed the city gaol until 1807. Much of the gaol was excavated from the rock below the wall and the only source of air was through pipes. 'In this frightful hole prisoners under sentence of death were confined – itself a living death', wrote Hemingway. It included

69 *The medieval Bridgegate was demolished in 1782 and replaced by this elegant classical arch, designed by the Chester architect Joseph Turner.*

a dreadful torture cell called Little Ease, which was only 1.3m (4$\frac{1}{2}$ft) high and 43cm (17in) wide at its greatest width. The height could be further reduced by inserting boards across the cell. A new gaol was built on open land near to the Infirmary to the design of the local architect Joseph Turner.

The Classical Revival: Chester Castle and the Grosvenor Bridge

Towards the end of the eighteenth century revived styles of architecture came into fashion. Architects travelled abroad to study Greek and Roman antiquities, and their findings were reproduced in buildings which strictly adhered to the classical orders. A number of these buildings were erected in Chester, notably William and Henry Brown's fashionable new shop in Eastgate Street, which opened in 1828. However, the greatest exponent of this style was undoubtedly Thomas Harrison (1744-1829), who worked in Chester for over forty years.

Harrison was a Yorkshireman who had studied architecture in Italy. In 1785 he won a

70 *Early nineteenth-century view of Thomas Harrison's Castle complex. St Bridget's church, in the foreground, was designed by Harrison's pupil, William Cole the younger, in 1828.*

competition to rebuild the county hall and gaol block at Chester Castle, which had fallen into a ruinous state. Between 1788 and 1822, Harrison created what Nikolaus Pevsner has described as '... one of the most powerful monuments of the Greek Revival in the whole of England' (**70**). The main block is of ashlared stone, with a central portico supported by six massive Doric columns. This contains the main courtroom, a semicircular chamber with a domed roof and Ionic columns. The wings to north and south contained the barrack blocks and armoury. The massive gateway, in the Doric order, flanked by two pedimented lodges, was the last part of Harrison's work, built between 1810 and 1822. It is said to have been inspired by the Propylaea at Athens and the Temple of Theseus.

Harrison's castle was not only an architectural masterpiece: it also included one of the most humane and enlightened prisons of its

103

day. According to the architectural historian Mark Girouard 'The architecture of Chester Castle symbolized to perfection the reforming spirit behind it'.

Thomas Harrison's other buildings in Chester include the Commercial Newsrooms in Northgate Street (1808), the Northgate (1808–10), Watergate House (1814) and his own home, St Martin's Lodge, built in 1820. By this time Harrison was already seventy-six years old. He had gained his first public appointment, county surveyor of Cheshire, only five years earlier. From the balcony of his new house, the elderly architect could enjoy an excellent view of Chester Castle and of his last work, the Grosvenor Bridge, begun in 1827 and completed three years after his death in 1832.

By the late eighteenth century the medieval Dee Bridge was no longer able to cope with the increased pressure of traffic. In 1818 Harrison was asked to submit plans for a second bridge. The design chosen was for a stone bridge with a span of 60m (200ft). In order to counter objectors who claimed that his vast stone arch would collapse, Harrison had a model made. It can be seen today in the embankment at Castle Drive. To provide access to the bridge, a new approach road, Grosvenor Street, was laid down in the late 1820s. It marked the first significant change to Chester's Roman and medieval street pattern and involved the demolition of many buildings, including the parish church of St Bridget, which was rebuilt at the junction of Grosvenor Street and Nicholas Street. It had stood on its original site in Bridge Street from Saxon times.

Wealthy suburbs, inner city slums

By the end of the Regency period, wealthier people were beginning to move away from the city centre. A fashionable new suburb of stuccoed villas grew up overlooking the river at Boughton. New streets like Egerton Street and Bold Square were laid out for the middle classes. In contrast, there were growing areas of extreme poverty, particularly along Frodsham Street, Love Street and adjacent to the canal. Behind the prosperous shopping streets large numbers of families were crowded into squalid courtyard dwellings. Over the next century the social conditions of the urban poor would be as much a problem in elegant Chester as they were in Liverpool and Manchester.

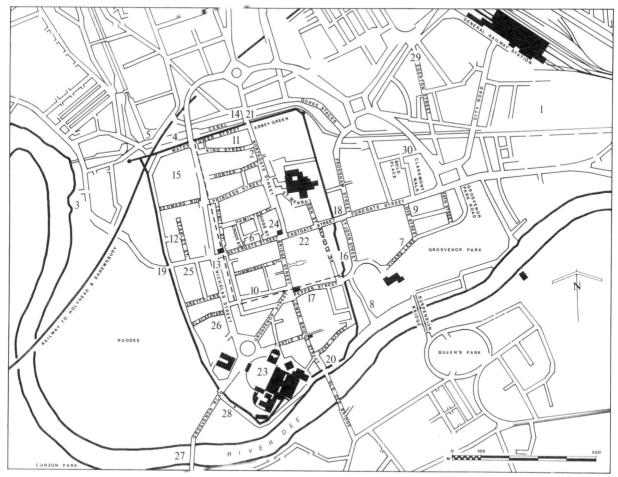

71 *Map of present-day Chester showing the location of Georgian and Regency buildings.*

1 *Leadworks shot tower*
2 *'Pied Bull'*
3 *Crane Wharf*
4 *Northgate locks*
5 *Tower Wharf canal basin*
6 *Booth Mansion*
7 *Former St John's Rectory*
8 *Old Bishop's Palace*
9 *Forest House*
10 *White Friars*
11 *King Street*
12 *Stanley Place*
13 *Nicholas Street*
14 *Blue Coat Hospital*
15 *Infirmary*

16 *Methodist Chapel, St John Street (interior)*
17 *Methodist Chapel, Pepper Street*
18 *Eastgate*
19 *Watergate*
20 *Bridgegate*
21 *Northgate*
22 *Brown's 'classical' building*
23 *The Castle*
24 *Commercial Newsrooms*
25 *Watergate House*
26 *St Martin's Lodge*
27 *Grosvenor Bridge*
28 *Model of the Grosvenor Bridge*
29 *Egerton Street*
30 *Bold Square*

105

9

Victorian and Edwardian Chester

Chester escaped the dramatic changes of fortune which transformed the great industrial cities of the north and Midlands during the reign of Queen Victoria; instead, the city enjoyed a period of steady growth and progress, during which it became firmly established as a major tourist centre and gained a legacy of distinctive buildings.

In the 1830s, Chester was still a prosperous county town, largely dependent upon its role as a retailing centre. While there was no large-scale manufacturing, a significant number of industries had grown up to the north of the city along the canal. The population was just over 21,000, and despite some movement to the suburbs, most people still lived, worked and died within the City Walls. By 1901, it had risen to more than 38,000 – a tiny increase compared with the major industrial towns but one which had a marked impact on the development of the city – and by Edwardian times there had been substantial suburban expansion.

The coming of the railways

During the 1840s, Chester was linked to the expanding rail network. The first lines to Birkenhead and Crewe opened in 1840, and over the next decade the city became an important railway centre, connected to London, Manchester, Birmingham and North Wales. The General Station was opened in 1848 (**72**); it was designed by the railway architect Francis

Thompson in collaboration with Robert Stephenson, engineer to the Chester and Holyhead Railway. In 1856, it was estimated that 140 people were employed there; 98 passenger trains and over 70 goods trains arrived and departed every day.

The growth of the suburbs

New suburbs grew up around the station to meet the needs of workers on the railway and in associated trades. Both Hoole and Newton to the north-west of the city were developed during the mid-nineteenth century. There was also considerable development of housing on the south bank of the river Dee, including the two wealthy residential areas of Curzon Park and Queen's Park. In 1852 Queen's Park was connected to the city by a suspension bridge over the river. This was replaced by the present suspension bridge in 1923.

Tourism

The railways firmly established Chester as a tourist centre. By the end of the eighteenth century the city was already attracting many visitors, who passed through Chester on their way to Ireland or during tours of North Wales. Now that people could travel quickly and cheaply, Chester developed as a place to visit in its own right. Many tourists came from abroad; a bilingual French and English guidebook was produced in 1851. The city became particularly popular with Americans, many of

whom landed at Liverpool and travelled by rail to London via Chester.

Many hotels were built in City Road, which was laid down as a new approach to the General Station early in the 1860s. The Queen Hotel dates from 1861, although it was destroyed by fire and had to be rebuilt the following year. Across the road, the Queen Commercial Hotel (now the Town Crier) opened in 1867. In Eastgate Street, the old Royal Hotel was rebuilt between 1863 and 1866. It was renamed the Grosvenor Hotel after the owner Richard Grosvenor, the second Marquess of Westminster (**73**).

Shops and trade

The ever-increasing numbers of visitors further enhanced Chester's reputation as a retailing centre. By the early years of the century, the main shopping street, Eastgate Street, was being compared to London's Regent Street. Browns store, founded by Susannah Brown in the late eighteenth century, expanded rapidly and became known as the 'Harrods of the North'. In 1858 Brown's opened their new imposing Crypt Buildings, designed in the

72 *The General Railway Station soon after it opened in 1848. Its Italianate facade was thought to be the longest in the world: it measured 350m (1160ft).*

fashionable Gothic style to harmonize with the thirteenth-century undercroft below. Nearby, Bolland's confectioners was to become famous as the supplier of Queen Victoria's wedding cake. Many shops began to sell souvenirs of Chester.

Chester's ancient fairs declined at the beginning of the century and their business began to be transacted in new commercial halls, built by Lancashire and Yorkshire merchants. Union Hall (1808) and Commercial Hall (1815) were on opposite sides of Foregate Street. Both were large quadrangular buildings, housing small shops on three tiers of galleries. Goods of every description could be purchased, wholesale and retail, under one roof. By the mid-nineteenth century Chester tradesmen were complaining that these 'foreign marts of commerce' were taking business away from their own shops.

The markets retained their regional importance, but there was growing concern that most goods were sold in insanitary conditions in the street. The main market was in Northgate

73 *The Grosvenor Hotel, designed by T.M. Penson, opened in Eastgate Street in 1866.*

Street in front of the Exchange. In the early 1860s, a competition was held to design a new covered market. The winner was James M. Hay of Liverpool, who produced a 'splendid and unique building with a jolly baroque facade'.

The Town Hall

In December 1862, the old Exchange was severely damaged by fire and had to be demolished. Another competition was held for designs for a new Town Hall. It was won by W.H. Lynn of Belfast. His High Victorian Gothic Town Hall was built between 1864 and 1869 and was opened amidst much celebration by the Prince of Wales, the future Edward VII (**colour plate 14**).

Churches

The Victorian passion for church restoration is very evident in Chester. The architect responsible for most of the work was James Harrison (1814–66) – no relation of Thomas Harrison –

a local man and son of a stonemason. During the 1840s and 1850s, Harrison was Chester's leading architect and chief exponent of the Gothic Revival in the city. In 1849–50 he completely rebuilt St Michael's Church in Bridge Street, introducing light-coloured stone from Minera near Wrexham in North Wales rather than the local red sandstone. Both St Peter's and St Mary's Churches were heavily restored, and in 1865–9 Holy Trinity Church in Watergate Street was rebuilt to his designs.

Chester Cathedral was also transformed in appearance by a succession of architects. By far the most dramatic alterations were made between 1868 and 1876 by Sir George Gilbert Scott. There was no question that major repairs were needed: Scott discovered that 'the external stonework was so horribly and lamentably decayed as to reduce it to a mere wreck, like a mouldering sandstone cliff'. However, Scott did far more than repair. He largely rebuilt the

Lady Chapel and added the turrets, pinnacles and flying buttresses which adorn the exterior. He wanted to add a tall central spire, but this was never executed. Most controversial was his reconstruction of the east end of the south choir aisle with a polygonal apse, for which Scott claimed to have found archaeological evidence. Scott's work was followed by that of C.J. Blomfield, who designed the former King's School on the site of the old Bishop's Palace in 1876, and Sir Giles Gilbert Scott, who restored the monastic buildings shortly before the First World War.

The 'Black and White Revival'

During the second half of the nineteenth century a group of local architects, working independently, effectively created Chester's black-and-white appearance. They were influenced by the timber-frame tradition which had characterized Cheshire's domestic buildings in medieval and Tudor times. They also made extensive use of brick and stone, but it is their half-timbered rebuilding which has become such a distinctive feature of Chester. According to Nikolaus Pevsner, 'Chester is not a medieval, it is a Victorian city. What deceives is the black and white 95 per cent is Victorian and after'. In fact, there was never any intention to deceive, and Chester's Victorian architects generally produced buildings of individuality, imagination and craftsmanship, which have earned the city a distinctive place in the history of late Victorian architecture.

By the 1850s there had been a national reaction against classical architecture. Feelings were particularly strong in Chester, where many ancient buildings had been lost through Georgian rebuilding and refacing. This spirit was typified by the determination shown by the Chester Architectural, Archaeological and Historical Society to 'save' God's Providence House in Watergate Street. In 1861, members were outraged by a proposal to demolish this small timber building of 1652. However, they were satisfied when the owner agreed to rebuild

in a similar style (**front cover**).

In fact, by 1861 the black-and-white revival was already well under way. Ten years earlier, another architect, T.M. Penson (1816–64), pioneered the style when he 'restored' a Mr Platt's pharmacist's shop in Eastgate Street. His work seems to have involved much rebuilding, but it won widespread approval. This building no longer exists, but in 1855–6 Penson built two gabled shops a few doors away (Nos 36 and 38 Eastgate Street). These were the first entirely new buildings of the revival.

The earliest of these new timber buildings were rather free and easy interpretations; later the form and detailing was to become far more convincing as architects made a careful study of medieval building techniques. Another Chester architect, T.M. Lockwood (1830–1900), became one of the ablest exponents of the new half-timbering, evolving a 'personal and recognizable style and distinctive manner of detailing'. His most famous buildings are the ornate group on the corner of Eastgate Street and Bridge Street at the Cross, built for the Duke of Westminster in 1888. Four years later, he combined half-timber with brick and stone in the buildings on the opposite side of the Cross, also for the Duke.

Chester's Victorian rebuilding was greatly influenced by the Grosvenor family, particularly Richard Grosvenor, second Marquess of Westminster and his successor the third Marquess, who became the first Duke of Westminster in 1874. During the century they embarked on a massive programme of building both in the city and on their vast Eaton Estate, employing all the leading local architects of the day.

The most noted and most prolific of these architects was undoubtedly John Douglas (1830–1911). He practised in the city for over fifty years, giving Chester many of its best-loved buildings. Douglas's buildings are always superbly detailed and display a strong sense of craftsmanship. Distinctive features of his work include beautifully carved timbers, romantic turrets, oriel windows, 'barley-sugar' chimneys

109

74 *Grosvenor Park Road, one of John Douglas's most successful compositions, was built in 1879/80.*

and the blue patterned brickwork which became the hallmark of most Eaton estate buildings.

Douglas's most famous black-and-white work in Chester includes Grosvenor Park Lodge (1865–7), St Paul's Church at Boughton (1876) and the Harp and Crown public house (now Liberty's) in Bridge Street (1900). Between 1895 and 1897 he produced the brilliant range of buildings on the east side of St Werburgh Street.

Like Chester's other Victorian architects, Douglas also worked eloquently in other materials, notably local red Ruabon brick. In Grosvenor Park Road (1879–80), he created a terrace of Tudor–Gothic houses (**74**). At the end of the terrace is a former Baptist church built in the Flemish style. A similar style was used for the Grosvenor Club (now the Midland Bank) of 1883. The same materials, although with minimal detailing, were used in Parker's Buildings (1888–9), a tenement block in Fore-gate Street and now a rare survivor of this building form. Nearby, in Bath Street, is one of Douglas's most imaginative developments, a picturesque terrace of tiny stone cottages with delightful round turrets, completed in 1903.

John Douglas died in 1911 at Walmoor Hill, Dee Banks, the house he had built for himself in 1896. Given the range and variety of his Chester buildings, it is somewhat ironic that his most famous structure should be a clock. The Eastgate Clock was erected in 1899 to commemorate the Diamond Jubilee two years earlier. Douglas designed the intricate wrought iron turret, which has since become a symbol of Chester all over the world.

With one notable exception, Chester's Victorian architects respected and preserved the Rows. The Victorian Rows are wider, lighter and airier than the originals, but they maintain the continuity and essential character of the ancient system. However, at the very end of the century, the medieval Shoemakers' Row on the west side of Northgate Street was demolished and redeveloped by a number of architects. The elevated Row walkway was completely lost, replaced by a black-and-white arcade just above street level. The last building in the range was completed in 1903 and has a canopied statue of the new king, Edward VII, facing Town Hall Square.

Black-and-white building continued throughout Edward's reign, and there was always fierce local support for the style. In 1910, part of Bridge Street was redeveloped as a shopping arcade by the second Duke of Westminster. The design by W.T. Lockwood was typically Edwardian Baroque, faced with white tiles. It was widely criticized because it did not fit in with the 'picturesque' character of the historic Rows and a year later it was refronted in timber. St Michael's Buildings, with its three massive half-timbered gables, contrasts sharply with Lockwood's original faience arcade which was allowed to survive behind.

Leisure

In the second half of the nineteenth century there was considerable interest in recreation and culture. Provision of this was aimed at all levels of society, and the chief benefactors were the Grosvenor family. Between 1865 and 1867, the second Marquess of Westminster commissioned the landscape architect Edward Kemp to lay out Grosvenor Park on some twenty acres of land overlooking the river. At the end of the century, the first Duke presented Edgar's Field in Handbridge to the city. The Groves, Chester's popular riverside promenade, was extended and improved in the 1880s at the expense of Alderman Charles Brown. From here, pleasure-boat trips to Eaton Hall became a popular tourist attraction.

By the 1880s, Chester had acquired its first free Public Library in St John Street. Until

75 *Sherratt's Art Gallery in Bridge Street, one of the most flamboyant of Chester's Victorian black-and-white buildings.*

1885 the museum was housed in the Water Tower on the City Walls, where attractions included a camera obscura. In that year the Grosvenor Museum was built by public subscription and named after its main benefactor. The architect was T.M. Lockwood. For lovers of art there were many private galleries, including Sherratt's Art Gallery in Bridge Street (**75**). The idiosyncratic black-and-white building, complete with biblical scenes and statue of King Charles I, is undoubtedly the most exuberant of the revival period.

Popular entertainment was provided by the

Music Hall which opened in the medieval St Nicholas's Chapel in 1855. It replaced the Theatre Royal, which had fallen from fashion in early Victorian times. The conversion was by James Harrison, who added the Tudor-style windows and porch to the new east front. Among the many stars who performed here was Charles Dickens, who enthralled audiences with impassioned readings from his own works in 1867.

Housing

Despite all the visible evidence of prosperity, extreme poverty and appalling housing conditions were as rife in Chester as in any other Victorian city. However, much of it was hidden from view, large numbers of Chester's working population being concentrated in the notorious 'courts' of slum housing which grew up behind the main streets. In 1851, 202 people were crowded into Parry's Court behind Foregate Street. By 1905, there were said to be 122 courts, containing 747 houses and a population of 2500 living in insanitary conditions. These were finally swept away in the 1930s.

Civic improvements

Following the Municipal Corporations Act which reformed local government in 1835, there were considerable civic improvements in Chester. Streets were resurfaced, new pavings laid down and improved drainage systems introduced. Gas light had been provided since 1817, when the city's first gasworks were established in Cuppin Street. Electricity was introduced at the end of the century, when a power station was erected in Crane Street. In 1913, the Corporation opened a supplementary hydro-electric power station by the Old Dee Bridge. The site had previously been occupied by the famous Dee Mills which were badly damaged by fire in 1895 and demolished in 1910.

Trams were an important feature of late Victorian and Edwardian Chester. The first horse-drawn service began in 1879, between the General Station and the industrial suburb of Saltney. The service was electrified in 1903 and the lines were extended to Boughton three years later. Inevitably, the trams became a popular visitor attraction and by the end of this period they were regarded as the best way to see Chester quickly and cheaply.

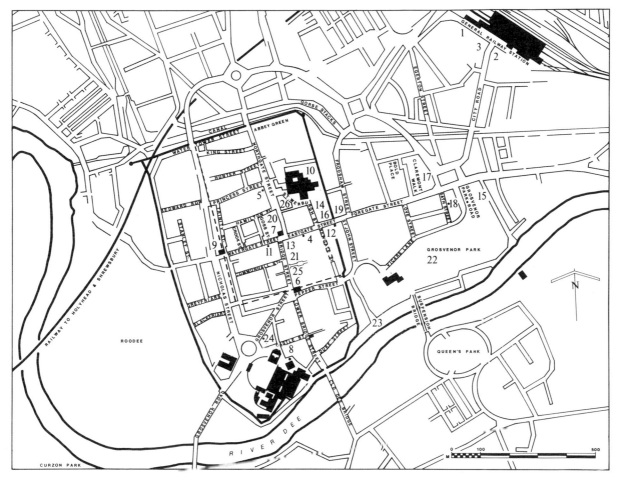

76 *Map of present-day Chester, showing the location of Victorian and Edwardian buildings.*

1 *General Railway Station*
2 *Queen Hotel*
3 *Queen Commercial Hotel (now the 'Town Crier')*
4 *Brown's Crypt Building*
5 *Town Hall*
6 *St Michael's Church (now the City Council Heritage Centre)*
7 *St Peter's Church*
8 *St Mary's Church*
9 *Holy Trinity Church*
10 *Cathedral*
11 *God's Providence House*
12 *Grosvenor Hotel*
13 *Black-and-white buildings at the Cross*
14 *Black-and-white buildings on eastern side of St Werburgh Street*
15 *Tudor–Gothic houses on Grosvenor Park Road*
16 *Flemish-style Grosvenor Club (now the Midland Bank)*
17 *Parker's Buildings*
18 *Turreted cottages in Bath Street*
19 *Eastgate Clock*
20 *Shoemakers' Row*
21 *St Michael's Buildings*
22 *Grosvenor Park*
23 *The Groves*
24 *Grosvenor Museum*
25 *Sherratt's Art Gallery*
26 *The Music Hall*

10

Chester in the Twentieth Century

In 1931, the Chester Guide Book noted: 'Throughout the whole course of history, Chester has been known all over the world for its antiquities. But it has also built up in recent times a reputation in directions other than those, and today it ranks as one of the most important railway centres in the country, and is noted for its varied and flourishing trades.' Despite this optimism, Chester never developed as a manufacturing town, although modern industries, most notably aerospace and chemicals, have grown up nearby. During the twentieth century, the city has lost most of its old-established industries. Instead, it has strengthened its position as a service centre, reflecting the city's regional importance in the fields of administration, retailing, commerce and tourism.

The port and canal
The demise of Chester's port, which had been widely predicted since Tudor times, did not finally happen until Connah's Quay docks closed in the 1960s. Steam coasters were still coming up to Crane Wharf until the early 1930s. Shipbuilding ended in 1935 when Crichton's yard at Saltney closed. The last sea-going vessel to be built at Chester was the Allegheny, an oil tanker of 856 tons. However, J. Taylor's boatyard, which moved to Tower Wharf canal basin in 1917, survives as a working yard.

Commercial carrying on the Shropshire Union Canal continued well after the Second World War. The main traffic was the carriage of bulk liquid cargoes from Stanlow oil refinery at Ellesmere Port to the chemical works at Oldbury on the Birmingham Canal Navigation. By the late 1950s, commercial activity had ceased and the large Dee Basin adjacent to the river was almost completely filled in. However, since the early 1970s Chester has benefited from the increased popularity of pleasure boating and the canal is now an important tourist attraction.

Traffic
Chester's importance as a provincial railway centre also declined after the Second World War. Both the Northgate and Liverpool Road stations had closed by 1970. However, motor traffic increased dramatically, and by the 1930s the city centre was constantly choked with cars: the Cross became a notorious bottle-neck. Plans for a ring road were made in the inter-war period, but only short sections were actually constructed. In the late 1930s part of Pepper Street was widened and a new bridge in the Walls, the Newgate, was built. At the beginning of this work, the Roman amphitheatre was discovered and the new road was diverted around it.

It was not until the completion of the Inner Ring Road in 1972 that the first steps were

taken to reduce traffic in the central areas. In the same year the Cross was closed to all vehicles except buses and emergency vehicles. Further improvements were made in 1981, when the City Council introduced a programme of pedestrianisation. Since then Eastgate Street, Northgate Street and parts of Town Hall Square have been pedestrianised and further phases are planned.

Housing and post-war development

At the end of the First World War, housing became a major issue. The City Council came under strong pressure to provide 'homes fit for heroes' in line with Lloyd George's 1918 general election slogan. New estates of municipal housing were developed at Buddicome Park, Heath Lane, Handbridge and Lache. Most of the new tenants came from the Princess Street area behind the Town Hall, where over 200 slum dwellings were cleared in the 1930s (**77**).

77 *Banners Court off Princess Street was demolished as part of the slum clearance programme of the 1930s.*

After the Second World War there was a further need to rehouse large numbers of people quickly. In 1945, a major redevelopment plan for Chester was produced by the City Engineer and Surveyor, Charles Greenwood. Greenwood's recommendations for housing were inspired by '... the desire to build a better and more ordered world, which shall create in the minds of the people a greater sense of happiness and security'. He envisaged the creation of 'neighbourhood units' – large estates with their own amenities, which could develop as self-contained communities. Blacon, to the west of Chester, was identified as ideal for development because 'The site is elevated and the air is the most bracing in the district'. In 1948 the Council began building 1000 houses at Blacon; this number was to increase to over 3000 by the 1970s.

115

78 *Charles Greenwood's post-war redevelopment plans included this proposal for a large concert hall which would have formed part of a formal Civic Centre around the Town Hall.*

79 *The Victorian Market Hall was demolished amidst fierce controversy in 1967.*

There were few significant changes to Chester's appearance until the 1960s. The city escaped any serious bomb damage during the Second World War. Greenwood's vision for post-war redevelopment, which included a formal civic centre around the Town Hall, never came to fruition (**78**). Even the 1960s brought little large-scale development, although that which did take place had a considerable impact on the appearance and historic remains of the city. The greatest change to the townscape was caused by the building of the Inner Ring Road, when many important Georgian buildings were lost. Chester also lost its much loved Victorian market hall when the area behind the Town Hall was redeveloped for the Forum Precinct, new market hall and Gateway Theatre (**79**). Other new developments were less obtrusive: the Grosvenor-Laing shopping precinct, set behind the Row buildings of Eastgate Street and Bridge Street, was thought to 'set an admirable standard for the future' when it opened in 1965.

Conservation

By the late 1960s Chester, like many other historic towns, was suffering from serious physical decay. Important buildings were in danger of collapse or threatened with redevelopment; whole areas such as Bridgegate were in decline. Donald W. Insall and Associates were invited to produce a comprehensive report on the problems facing Chester. *Chester: A Study in Conservation* was published in 1968 and became the blueprint for an ambitious Conservation Programme which continues today. Since 1969, over 600 historic buildings have been restored and Chester has won numerous awards, including the prestigious Europa Nostra Award on two occasions.

80 *Sympathetic modern infill buildings at Heritage Court behind Lower Bridge Street.*

Chester's determination to hold on to the past has generally been reflected in its twentieth-century buildings. The black-and-white revival continued well into the 1920s. With the exception of Harry Weedon's Odeon cinema, the 1930s produced few buildings of note. Post-war modernism failed to find popular favour in Chester: both St Martin's Gate (1966) and the County Police Headquarters (1967) aroused fierce controversy when they were built. More recently, the desire to design buildings which are sympathetic to the existing character of the city has tended to produce replica facades or buildings which rely heavily on design details from the past (**80**).

Chester today

Chester's historic importance as a shopping and tourist centre has not declined. The city is ranked as one of the most successful provincial shopping centres in the country and welcomes over five million visitors every year. The city centre is noted for its small specialist shops, many still concentrated in the Rows; it has also attracted most of the leading national multiple stores. Tourism has grown into a major industry and Chester is promoted all over the world. It is a popular base for touring North Wales. Chester Zoo, founded in the 1930s, is one of the largest in the country and a major tourist attraction in its own right.

The Chester of today has evolved from nearly 2000 years of history. The visible evidence is everywhere: in the City Walls and other archaeological remains; in the wealth of historic buildings reflecting almost every age and architectural style; in the Cathedral (**colour plate 15**) and many fine churches; and in the collections of the Grosvenor Museum. Ancient traditions have been kept alive. Chester still hosts the oldest horse races in the country on the Roodee; the famous Mystery Plays continue to be performed every five years; the Lord Mayor of Chester still holds the ancient title of Admiral of the Dee. Yet the city is not a museum-piece. While respecting and preserving the past, Chester continues to develop as a modern and vibrant city of character and individuality (**colour plate 16**).

Further Reading

The literature on the history and archaeology of Chester, as of many of our historic towns, is large and growing. Much of it is only accessible in specialist publications. Here we attempt to guide readers to standard works with good bibliographies and to a few essential recent discussions. Some of the older books may be difficult to obtain except through larger libraries and, although they remain useful collections of information, the views expressed in them have often been superseded.

History, archaeology and architecture – general

Borsay, P. (ed.) *The Eighteenth-Century Town, 1688–1820*, London & New York: Longman, 1990

Cruikshank, D. *A Guide to the Georgian Buildings of Britain and Ireland*, London: Weidenfeld & Nicholson, 1985

Cruikshank, D. & Burton, N. *Life in the Georgian City*, London: Viking, 1990

Darvill, T. *Prehistoric Britain*, London: Batsford, 1987

Frere, S.S. *Britannia: a history of Roman Britain*, 3rd ed., London: Routledge & K.P., 1987

Girouard, M. *The English Town*, London and New Haven: Yale University Press, 1990

Hill, D. *An Atlas of Anglo-Saxon England*, Oxford: Blackwell, 1981

Jones, G.D.B. & Mattingly, D. *An Atlas of Roman Britain*, Oxford: Blackwell, 1990

Millett, M. *The Romanization of Britain*, Cambridge U.P., 1990

Salway, P. *Roman Britain*, Oxford U.P., 1981

Stenton, F.M. *Anglo-Saxon England*, 3rd ed., Oxford U.P., 1971

History and archaeology of Chester and Cheshire – general

Higham, N.J. *The Origins of Cheshire*, Manchester U.P., 1993

Sylvester, D. & Nulty, G. *The Historical Atlas of Cheshire*, Chester: Cheshire Community Council, 1958

Volumes of the *Victoria County History*, published by the Oxford University Press for the London University Institute of Historical Research:

Harris, B.E. (ed.) *A History of the County of Chester*, vol. 3, 1980

Thacker, A.T. (ed.) *A History of the County of Chester*, vol. 1, 1987

Harris, B.E. *Chester*, Edinburgh: Bartholomew, 1979 (Bartholomew City Guides)

Kennett, A.M. (ed.) *Chester: 1900 Years of History*, Chester City Council, 1979

Kennett, A.M. (ed.) *Chester and the River Dee*, Chester City Council, 1982

Palliser, D.M. (ed.) *Chester: contemporary descriptions by residents and visitors*, 2nd ed., Chester City Council, 1980

Pevsner, N. & Hubbard, E. *The Buildings of England: Cheshire*, Harmondsworth: Penguin, 1971

The Cheshire landscape

Furness, R.R. *Soils of Cheshire*, Harpenden, 1978 (Soil Survey Bulletin 6)

Cheshire in prehistory

Varley, W.J. *Cheshire before the Romans*, Cheshire Community Council, 1964

Roman Chester

Carrington, P. 'The Roman advance into the northwestern midlands before AD 71' *Journal of the Chester Archaeological Society* 68, 1985, 5–22

Carrington, P. 'The plan of the Roman legionary fortress at Chester: a reconsideration' *J. Chester Archaeol. Soc.* 68, 1985, 23–51

Carrington, P. 'The plan of the legionary fortress at Chester: further comparisons' *J. Chester Archaeol. Soc.* 69, 1986, 7–17

Mason, D.M. 'The extra-mural area' In: Strickland, T.J. & Davey, P.J. (eds) *New Evidence for Roman Chester*, Liverpool University, 1978, 29–40

Mason, D.M. 'The *prata legionis* at Chester' *J. Chester Archaeol. Soc.* 69, 1986, 19–43

Mason, D.M. *Excavations at Chester, 11–15 Castle Street and Neighbouring Sites 1974–8*, Chester City Council, 1980

Thompson, F.H. *Roman Cheshire*, Cheshire Community Council 1965

Thompson, F.H. 'The excavation of the Roman amphitheatre at Chester' *Archaeologia* 105, 1976, 127–239

Roman pottery

Bulmer, M. 'An introduction to Roman samian ware' *J. Chester Archaeol. Soc.* 62, 1979, 5–72

Carrington, P. 'Roman pottery in Chester' In: Ward, S. *Excavations at Chester, 12 Watergate Street 1985: Roman headquarters building to medieval Row*, Chester City Council, 1988, 18–21

Holt

Blockley, K. 'The Roman-British period' in: Manley, J. *et al.* (eds) *The Archaeology of Clwyd*, Clwyd County Council, 1991, 117–28

Greene, K.T. 'Legionary pottery and the significance of Holt'. In: *Roman Pottery Studies in Britain and Beyond*, Oxford: British Archaeological Reports International Series 30, 1977, 113–32

Grimes, W.F. 'Holt, Denbighshire, the works-depot of the Twentieth legion at Castle Lyons' *Y Cymmrodor* 41, 1930

Stephens, G.R. 'Roman Holt: personnel, production and water supply' *Transactions of the Denbighshire Historical Society* 33, 1984, 81–92

Roman inscriptions from Chester

Collingwood, R.G. & Wright, R.P. *The Roman Inscriptions of Britain*, Oxford U.P., 1965

Keppie, L. *Understanding Roman Inscriptions*, London: Batsford, 1991

Richmond, I.A. & Wright, R.P. *The Roman inscribed and sculptured stones in the Grosvenor Museum, Chester* Chester Archaeological Society, 1955

Dark Age and Saxon Chester

Alldridge, N.J. 'The topography of early medieval Chester', *J. Chester Archaeol. Soc.* 64, 1981, 5–31

Bu'lock, J.D. *Pre-Conquest Cheshire 383–1066* Cheshire Community Council, 1972

Higham, N.J. 'Northumbria, Mercia and the Irish Sea, 893–926' in: Graham-Campbell, J. (ed.) *Viking Treasure from the North-west*, Liverpool Museum, 1992, 21–30

Griffiths, D. 'The coastal trading ports of the Irish Sea' In: Graham-Campbell, J., *op. cit.*, 63–72

Mason, D.M. *Excavations at Chester, 26–42 Lower Bridge Street 1974–6: The Dark Age and Saxon periods*, Chester City Council, 1985

Ward, S.W. *Excavations at Chester, Saxon Occupation within the Roman Fortress: sites excavated 1971–1981*, Chester City Council (forthcoming)

The Saxon mint

Blackburn, M.A.S. (ed.) *Anglo-Saxon Monetary History: essays in memory of Michael Dolley*, Leicester U.P., 1986

Pirie, E.J.E. *The Willougby Gardner Collection of Coins with the Chester Mint Signature. Sylloge of Coins of the British Isles, Volume 5 – the Grosvenor Museum, Chester*, Part 1. London: British Academy, 1964

Medieval Chester – general

Beck, J. *Tudor Cheshire*, Cheshire Community Council, 1969

Dodgson, J.McN. 'Place-names and street-names of Chester', *J. Chester Archaeol. Soc.*, 55, 1968, 29–62

Dodgson, J.McN. *The Place-Names of Cheshire Part Five (Section 1:1)*, Cambridge U.P., 1981

Driver, J.T. *Cheshire in the Later Middle Ages*, Cheshire Community Council, 1971

Hewitt, H.J. *Cheshire under the Three Edwards*, Cheshire Community Council, 1967

Husain, B.M.C. *Cheshire under the Norman Earls*, Cheshire Community Council, 1973

Morris, R.H. *Chester in the Plantagenet and Tudor Reigns*, Chester: privately printed [1894]

The Castle

Colvin, H.M. (ed.) *The History of the King's Works: vol 2, the Middle Ages*, London: HMSO, 1963

St Werburgh's Abbey

Burne, R.V.H. *Chester Cathedral*, London: S.P.C.K., 1958

Burne, R.V.H. *The Monks of Chester*, London: S.P.C.K., 1962

The religious houses

Ward, S.W. *Excavations at Chester, the Lesser Medieval Religious Houses: sites investigated 1964–1983*, Chester City Council, 1990

The Rows

Kennett, A.M. (ed.) 'Galleries which they call the Rows' *J. Chester Archaeol. Soc.* 67, 1984

Willshaw, E. *Chester's Rows*, Chester City Council (forthcoming)

The Chester leather industry

Kowaleski, M. 'Town and country in late medieval England: the hide and leather trade' in: Corfield, P.J. & Keene, D. (eds) *Work in Towns 850–1850*, Leicester U.P., 1990, 55–73

Woodward, D.M. 'The Chester leather industry' *Transactions of the Historical Society of Lancashire & Cheshire* 119, 1968, 65–111

The Civil War siege

Dore, R.N. *The Civil War in Cheshire*, Cheshire Community Council, 1966

Kennett, A.M. (ed.) *Loyal Chester: a brief history of Chester in the Civil War period*, Chester City Council, 1984

Ward, S.W. *Excavations at Chester, the Civil War Siegeworks 1642–6*, Chester City Council, 1987

Restoration Chester

Hill, C. *The Century of Revolution, 1603–1714*, 2nd ed., London: Van Nostrand, 1980

Hodson, J.H. *Cheshire 1660–1780: Restoration to industrial revolution*, Cheshire Community Council, 1978

Georgian Chester

Anon *The Modest Genius: Thomas Harrison*, Chester City Council, 1977

Hemingway, J. *History of the City of Chester*, 2 vols, Chester: Fletcher, 1831

Kennett, A.M. (ed.) *Georgian Chester*, Chester City Council, 1987

Victorian Chester

Audsley, G.A. *Guide to Chester*, Chester: Catherall & Pritchard, 1898

Audsley, G.A. *The Stranger's Handbook to Chester*, revised ed., Chester: Phillipson & Golder, 1908

Hargreaves, C. 'Social areas within the Walls of Chester, 1861' *J. Chester Archaeol. Soc.* 65, 1982

Hubbard, E. *The Work of John Douglas*, London: Victorian Society, 1991

Hughes, T. *The Stranger's Handbook to Chester and its Environs*, Chester: Catherall and Pritchard, 1856

Chester in the twentieth century

Insall, D.W. *Chester: a study in conservation*, London: H.M.S.O., 1968

Insall, D.W. & Morris, C. *Conservation in Chester*, Chester City Council

Greenwood, C. *Chester: a plan for redevelopment*, Chester City Council,

Tigwell, R.E. *Cheshire in the Twentieth Century*, Cheshire Community Council, 1985

Glossary

Camera obscura A dark room in which images of outside objects are projected on to a screen from a long-focus lens using natural light.

'Celtic fields' Small rectangular fields, defined by banks and often arranged in regular patterns. They vary from 0.1ha ($^1/_4$ acre) to 0.6ha ($1^1/_2$ acres) in area. Many appear to originate in the Roman period or earlier.

Cohort An infantry unit of the Roman army, consisting of either 500 or 1000 men. Legions had ten cohorts, all made up of six centuries and about 500 strong, except for the senior First Cohort, which was double strength in the late first century.

Doric The oldest and plainest of the three orders of Greek architecture, distinguished by the lack of a base to the columns and the very simple decoration on the capitals and entablature above.

Faience Glazed and painted tiles.

'Gothic Revival' A movement to revive the Gothic style of architecture in the late eighteenth and nineteenth centuries; applied especially to churches

Hypocaust Under-floor ducts for hot air used in the Roman system of central heating.

Ionic One of the orders of Greek architecture, distinguished by columns with half-round mouldings on the bases and flat capitals decorated with large spiral scrolls.

Nonconformist A Protestant body separated from the Church of England.

Oriel A bay window projecting from the upper floor only of a building.

Palatine A county or its feudal ruler with independence of the Crown in judicial matters.

Palstave A form of axe-head common during the Middle Bronze Age (c. 1750–1250 BC). It fitted into a slot cut in the end of an L-shaped handle and had side-flanges and a cross-ridge to locate it.

Prothonotary The chief clerk of a court.

Roving bridge A bridge over a canal, built with spiral approach ramps to allow a horse to cross from one tow path to the other without having to drop the tow rope.

Sallyport A small gateway between the inner and outer works of a fortification.

Vexillation An element, often 1000 strong (i.e. two cohorts), detached from a legion and serving under its own standard (*vexillum*), either independently or together with similar detachments from other legions.

Index